Who Am I?

*A Woman's Journey of Transformation
from a Child of the Flesh to a Child of God*

Elaina Lee Richter

ISBN 979-8-88685-264-6 (paperback)
ISBN 979-8-88685-265-3 (digital)

Christian Faith Publishing
832 Park Avenue
Meadville, PA 16335
www.christianfaithpublishing.com

Printed in the United States of America

CONTENTS

CHAPTER 1

Childhood

August 14, 1997

I watched the bumblebee going about its way, landing on each flower, gently swaying in the breeze, then moving on to the next one and the next before flying off to another world. I wondered how one of God's creatures, so gentle and pure, felt to be able to fly. Fly off into different places, different worlds, and free to do as he pleases. As he flew off, I knew things would be better for him. A different area, different flowers, and a different life. I had a warm feeling for him as a smile tried to form on my face under the tears. I moved on. I walked a little way up. The smell of summer heat, cooled slightly by a gentle breeze, and the taste of green grass and blooming flowers filled the air as I walked up the hill toward my favorite place.

I took one leap to the other side, and what had once seemed liked a canyon now seemed like a crack. I climbed the rocks over the ditch and was halted by a slug. I observed him for a minute and started to envy him. How come he got to stay? He was able to stay on the rock that I had spent most of my childhood days playing on—those days when make-pretend and imagination were your life, and your life was pure happiness. He was able to stay in his home he's had all his life and that wasn't fair to me. I wanted to kill him, but that would just deny him the life I wish I was going to have, so I left.

I stepped across the ditch and saw it. There it was, gently rocking with each little gust, the old wooden swing my dad had put up when I was born. I sat in it one more time, afraid it might break. After all, I wasn't the small child who used to swing up to the sky, let my imagination run wild, and close my eyes and begin to fly. No, that wasn't me anymore. The seat was too hard, and it was getting me dirty. I looked at the swing and felt bad for it. It had no choices; it was staying behind, and who knows what would happen to it. It might get taken down and just thrown out. I would hate to be treated like that, so I gave it a kiss as another tear came rolling down my face.

As I walked up the hill, along the side of my house up toward the woods, I stopped in my tracks as I stepped on something unusual. I looked down and under my feet was a patch of discolored grass and a piece of cement sticking up. I completely forgot we ever had a sandbox and didn't even remember we let it grow over. I felt sad for the sandbox because I was afraid that is what this would all become to me, completely forgotten and grown over. I was starting to grow up, and I was scared. I was scared of the future and scared of forgetting my past. I wasn't ready to leave. I was scared this sandbox would represent the childhood I once knew. I moved on, up toward the woods.

I passed the shed my father built, the one I used to play on during hide-and-seek, and our pool, where I used to spend hours, days, and nights gliding in it, thinking how things couldn't get any better. It was true because they've only gotten worse. I would soon be leaving my childhood.

I passed our old raspberry bush, always covered in beetles and so it was a race to get the two that weren't already eaten. Behind it used to be the old hutch my father built for our guinea pigs to stay in over the summer. I approached the woods and walked through them. They were so big to me as a child, like an endless playground where I would spend hours building forts, running on all fours like a tiger, and hanging from the trees like a monkey. What used to seem like hours only took me three minutes—climbing over the rock path, past our fort, and finally reaching my old elementary school. We were so close, and I remember always playing tag and football and wishing I could just run right home. I was angry then, and I am angry now.

Why couldn't I just be free to go where I wanted? I walked around the fields and the playground, where for years I played cops and robbers, basketball, Wiffle ball, talked to friends on the swings, ogled at the boys, and stood against the wall when I got in trouble for hitting some annoying boy. I laughed to myself and moved on.

I took a different way back through the woods and came to the little bridge on the other side of the yard. I stood on one side of it for a minute and realized in just a few minutes, I would be crossing a different bridge—a bridge to a whole new life and a whole new world. This bridge represented a milestone in my life as I realized my childhood was over and I would soon be entering my life as a teenager. I started crossing the bridge as I remembered pretending to fish with sticks and leaves in the creek and making pretend food with dirt and mud, and the tears came down faster. This was it. I was almost to the end—the end of my childhood. I walked down the hill, passed our red brick wishing well, passed the stump my brothers and I used for home plate in our Wiffle ball games, and jumped off the ledge onto our driveway. I looked up at the net. Late-night games with my brothers were some of our greatest memories, getting so angry when the game ended because our ball rolled down our steep driveway and into the dark woods across the street. We had fun. It was perfect.

As I look at my house one last time, I slowly got in the car with tears in my eyes. We pulled out of the driveway we used to sled down when it was covered with snow, and I wiped away my tears, kept my head forward, and prepared myself to fly away just like that bumblebee to a different area, different flowers, and a different world.

*****

My relationship with God started back as long as I can remember. Looking back, it was more like a one-sided friendship; but nevertheless, there was something there. I was raised Catholic by my mother, baptized as a baby, attended church pretty regularly, and was involved with the youth group through my confirmation in eighth grade. I knew God was the Father, Jesus was the Son, and somewhere in there was a Holy Spirit, which I was a little unsure of, but I believed in them. After confirmation, I stopped attending church because I didn't feel like I was gaining anything by going, and it seemed more like a chore rather than a calling. I didn't feel I needed to confess my sins to another person when I could just speak to God myself. I prayed sometimes, but it was more to ask for things I wanted, like keeping family members healthy, to get a boyfriend, or for good weather on the day of our town carnival. I always asked a lot, but not ever thinking about what I could be giving to Him.

When things went my way, I rejoiced in God's plan; but when they didn't, I broke down, got angry, anxious, sad, or depressed over whatever it was. I didn't keep in touch with this "friend" or higher power regularly. I clearly didn't trust Him, and I didn't have daily conversations with Him to build that trust because I figured if I was a good person, why wasn't I happy all the time? I never asked how He was doing, or what I could be doing for Him. The relationship had been there maybe since I was six or seven years old, but it was only when I needed something, only on my terms, when I remembered to reach out, or when I wasn't too busy or completely exhausted. If I was Him and we were just friends, I would have cut me out of His life because it was a selfish, one-sided relationship, and I wouldn't want a friend like that.

I always thought I had a pretty good childhood. I had a mother, father, and two older brothers, Ron and Evan. Ron is two-and-a-half years older than me, and Evan is my half brother from my father's first marriage and is ten years older than me. Evan stayed with us during the week and left to go to his mom's on the weekends. We lived in a small house in an old neighborhood among a wealthy town, but it was set on an acre of property that seemed like an endless jungle to a child growing up. We had what we needed, and I had fun. My parents raised us with good morals, values and beliefs, and provided for us, while also making us earn things so we never felt spoiled and learned to appreciate the different things and opportunities that were given to us as my father continued climbing in his profession.

My mom had a huge heart. She went out of her way to do sweet and caring things for us. I would get a back rub on some nights while she sang "You Are My Sunshine" as I fell asleep. She didn't play with us much, but when she could, she took us to fun places. Sometimes, she would have a job, and I would have to go to day care or summer camp, which I hated at first, but then warmed up after a few days and ended up loving it. Other times, she was home with us and took us to the town beach on nice days; or if it were a rainy day, she would take us bowling or to the movies. We always had fun in the summers. We went to tag sales on Saturday mornings, and I got to get new toys, then we would run errands, and I was just fascinated with the idea of a card you could just buy things with without paying cash! When we were really lucky about once a year, she would take Ron and I on a shopping spree at Toys R Us. Those were some of my favorite memories.

My dad was probably like most dads during that time. He worked in the city and got home at six every night, ate dinner with us, then turned on the news and fell asleep on the couch shortly after. We would tease him about it, but he always said he was just looking at the back of his eyelids. He didn't engage much with us during the week, but some weekends when he wasn't doing yard work, he would take us fishing or other outdoorsy activities. When I was six, my parents purchased a lot in Vermont, where my dad would spend the next two years building a house from the ground up himself. We got to go up there with him on those weekends but had to entertain our-selves while he was hard at work. I remember when we just had the foundation and the floor of the first floor complete, my brother and I had to sit on this tiny couch in the middle of winter, wrapped up in sleeping bags, hats, and mittens, with a tiny space heater pointed toward us and a small old antenna television that got one channel on it while he worked during the day. The first year we got to at least go back and sleep at a local motel at night, which was fun. Eventually, we slept there even on the plywood. The best was one night when a bat was flying around where Ron and I were trying to sleep, and it took about an hour of screaming, brooms, and coats to eventually get him out. They were some of our greatest memories growing up though. The memories only grew better once the house was finally complete in 1992, and we thought we were the luckiest kids alive to have a vacation home. My dad showed us a lot of neat stuff and provided us with many great adventures, but the relationship never really went beyond activities together.

I grew up idolizing my older brothers. Ron and I fought like typical siblings, but we also did so much together. We played video games, sports, and used our imaginations to come up with the weirdest games around the house that probably drove our mother crazy by making a mess, like Double Dare obstacle courses and fishing with a hanger and a rope over our foyer railing for different objects of clothing down below. Almost every night, we played animal wrestling in our living room, where we had to pretend to be an animal and wrestle how that animal wrestled. He won every time, except when I turned into a fishing cat. I have no idea what kind of strength came over me when I was the fishing cat, but I beat him every time with that character. On weekends, we would wait for our parents to put us to bed, and then after they went to bed, I would sneak out and go sleep in his room, and we would just talk about silly things. I still wonder if our parents knew we were doing that and just let us think we were sneaking around. During long car trips to Vermont, we played something called "foot wrestling," which you can imagine almost always ended up with one of us getting kicked in the face and crying. When our parents were lucky, we played a less violent game, where we tried to make each other laugh, and there were a few staples that worked every time.

Evan and I had a big age gap, but we were most alike. We both despised green vegetables and held on to that commonality until he finally grew out of it in adulthood. I still do not eat green vegetables to this day, so I resent him a little for turning over to the light and onto the healthy side of life. We also loved art and music, and he introduced me to all the classic rock bands of the time, whom I still love to this day. He was the funniest guy I knew. His sense of humor was teasing and sarcastic, something I certainly picked up on over the years and still hold onto myself. He definitely played a huge part in shaping me to be the person I am today because he was around more than my father, and I looked up to him in everything I did.

As much as my brothers played with me, I was still the baby girl and longed for my mommy to play with me. I can't recall if she ever did, but because of that, I learned to have an imagination, be independent, and played all day long on my own and had a blast. I pretended to be different animals a lot, galloping around out in the yard. I wonder what I must have looked like to someone watching in. Probably pretty silly, but I had a passion for animals and an imagination that ran wild. I had no choice. There were no devices back then. We didn't get many television channels. We didn't have a swing set or a trampoline or a zip line to keep us occupied. I cut off branches to bushes and used them to pretend I had a tail. I had imaginary friends I made mud pies with. I talked to myself out loud and had full dialogues and put on one-man plays. I could be gone from morning until dinner outside, exploring the nature around us, and my mother would have no idea. That is how we did things back then. There were no worries about predators lurking or danger in the woods around our house. Our house was surrounded by woods and creeks and so many cool places to explore I didn't need anything except nature and an imagination. We had a homecooked meal each night, separate bedrooms, and clean clothes. My parents had us involved in sports and all the activities you can imagine. They loved us, and we had fun.

There was a lot of discipline. I loved my mom more than anything, but she disciplined hard. Strangling, slaps to the face and bottom, pinning me down on the bed, and yelling and beating. I don't remember a lot about the circumstances, but one time, vividly in my mind, was when we were out at a tag sale, and it was at a previous preschool teacher's house. I was too shy to say goodbye to her, and my mom was so angry she had her hand around my neck the entire car ride home, and the beating continued in my bedroom after we got home. I learned my shyness was not an acceptable trait, so I had to learn some other way around it.

Another time I was playing with a friend in my neighborhood, and she became annoyed that I was beating her at a game. She went up to my mom and told her I was cheating and calling her names, which was a lie, and later that day, I got a similar beating without even listening to my side of the story. I learned to be a pushover because no matter what my side of the story was, I wouldn't have a strong enough voice to actually be heard.

I am sure much of the discipline was warranted as I am not claiming to be a perfect child. But I started learning sometimes the simplest practices or mistakes earned me a rosy red cheek or a sore bottom. I learned how to walk on eggshells around my parents, and so I learned how to run and hide every time I thought I did something wrong, thinking somehow I could escape if I just hid in my closet for a few hours, hoping it would be forgotten. As I got older, the physical punishment dwindled, but it then began to seem like nothing I did was good enough. I was no longer trying to escape punishment but rather seeking praise and acceptance. My brother, however, seemed like he could do no wrong, so I constantly strived to be perfect like him.

I started doing anything I could to be more like my brother in the eyes of my mom. I learned how to people-please as a means of survival. Whatever I had to give up of myself would be worth it to make others happy and pleased with me. I tried to celebrate the little wins as they occurred, but when a loss would occur and I was punished, it made it harder to see the good in the wins or see them as wins at all. It was harder to give myself credit and keep going strong on my journey. If I got a B I was proud of, my brother would bring home an A, and my small win quickly became a loss in my parents' eyes. It seemed like no matter how hard I tried, I could see there was some disappointment there. I learned to value other's approval and acceptance over my own and strived endlessly to always do the best job and the right thing as a means of survival. I often would get in trouble for things I didn't even do while hanging out with others, so sometimes, it was easier to avoid others or situations where I could possibly get into trouble. I learned avoidance as a means of survival.

As I got a little older, I thought if I couldn't get my parents approval, then I would start looking elsewhere. As early as third grade, I remember starting to think of myself as a sexual being. I loved my male third-grade teacher and always strived to be the teacher's pet. He seemed to really like me as well, and I was always winning prizes and getting to ride in his car when we went on field trips. Each morning, he would hide a Lego man somewhere in the room, and we would have to find him. Whoever he called would get a prize, and more often than others, I was called. I felt so special when he picked me to take home the class Guinea Pig over summer break. I loved the attention and feeling like the favorite for once.

In fourth grade, this boy Kevin put his arm around me one day at lunch and walked me around like I belonged to him. I felt special being wanted by someone, and it felt good, so I started chasing boys. I learned how to be funny and flirty with boys, and my confidence started growing in male attention. In fifth grade, I had another male teacher. This one was much older. Sometimes, during tests, he would come around and start rubbing my back and shoulders. He leaned really close to my face to check my work. One time after I had sliced my finger in class, he came to my locker to check on me and put his hands on my shoulders and kissed me on the head. Was that weird? I wasn't sure. I felt attractive and special that the teacher paid so much attention to me even though I felt a little uncomfortable.

From there on out, I couldn't concentrate on anything but boys. I needed to be wanted. I craved it. I had three boys who had asked me to a dance that year in fifth grade, and I said yes to all of them. I felt so proud and wanted that I went through with it without telling any of them about the others. By the end of the night, I had to make a decision, so I ended up with the bad boy, which meant I had to break the hearts of the other two good guys. I did feel a little bad about it afterward, but I had the popular guy for a moment in time and felt like the popular girl for a moment, so it was going to turn out okay. I started having fantasies about my teachers and other older male figures in my life over the next few years. They all focused on me being taken advantage of in a classroom setting. It is what turned me on as early as middle school. I didn't have the acceptance in other areas, so I longed for it in a sexual situation.

I certainly wasn't running with the popular crowd in school at that time, but I had several really good friends and was a generally happy child. There were many times I was the target of teasing and bullying as we were a lower-class family in a very upper-class town outside of the city. I also was a strange girl, especially when I decided to get the short bowl haircut the summer after sixth grade, which brought on much more teasing and new rejection from my male peers as I, myself, looked like a little boy now. I certainly knew what the pain of rejection felt like at home and school, but I was also quick to forgive. No matter what I felt, the need to fit in and be accepted was stronger because I just wanted peace and happiness in my life, and those were the only ways I knew how to achieve them.

During the summer before seventh grade, I decided to join the youth group at my Catholic church. I'm not sure if I joined because my mom pushed me into it or if it was because my friend was joining, but I liked trying new things, and it seemed like something good I could be doing. The kids involved were very nice and welcoming. It wasn't something I was used to at school. Soon, I found myself attending all the activities and making wonderful new friends of all ages. It made me somewhat excited to go to church on Sundays because I was there for all kinds of activities anyway, so it was neat to be involved.

One night, the following summer, I started getting a series of harassing instant messages from one of the monsignors whom I really liked and looked up to. He led the boys of the youth group, and so somehow, he got wind that I liked one of them, thus started a chat back and forth, telling me I needed to stay away from him, and he didn't like me and said other bullying remarks about who I was. I was confused and shocked at the time as to why one of the monsignors would even have instant messenger in the first place and then to bully me online out of nowhere. It was someone in the church I liked and trusted, and this caused me to take a step back and pull away from something I really enjoyed—something that allowed me to escape from the bullying I endured at school. I was at such a pivotal moment in my life and faith and actually had found a new sense of peace and joy from my church involvement, so I didn't understand how God could allow one of his workers to hurt me like that, so I became angered. Of course, I never said anything to anyone at the church because I knew no one would believe me, especially when it involved a church official.

It didn't really matter, however, because that summer, my parents delivered me with the devastating news that we would be moving to Pennsylvania. That was three states away. My whole world, my whole life as I had known it to be, was about to change all within a couple of months. I had no choice in the matter. My opinion meant nothing. The decision had already been made behind my back, and I just had to accept it. I also had to accept my oldest brother would not be coming with us. He was my hero. We did everything together. We had so much in common, even though we were ten years apart. He made me laugh when I was feeling down. He played with me when no one else would. What would I do without him now? How does he feel now that his family would be leaving him? Would he be mad at me that I wasn't staying? The anxiety felt unbearable at times as the questions bombarded my mind constantly.

I prayed a lot that night. I looked to God out of desperation, even though I was angry with Him. I begged Him not to let us move, to figure out a different way. I loved my house, my friends, and my town. I had no idea what else was out there, and I didn't want to know. I didn't have the greatest life in school, but I was comfortable with what I already knew. I liked being able to ride my bike down to the center of town each day during the summer and go to the pharmacy to buy little toys or to the video store to rent a movie for myself that night. We had just gotten our swimming pool the summer before, and it was the best thing in the world for a kid who didn't have a lot. I knew nothing about Pennsylvania. Did it have three lakes within five minutes of my house I could go to the beach each day to? It didn't help. August 14 came, and I was forced to say goodbye to my childhood as I knew it. My prayers went unanswered.

CHAPTER 2

Adolescence

September 5, 1999

Wow, I thought a lot today and discovered many new things about myself. I've been hurt in the past few months with guys. I was falling way too quickly, even before I knew them, like Jeremy. I totally gave myself away and ended up being a total dork, begging him to go places. From now on, I am making a pact. I am not going out with someone until I know them for at least a month. No guy is right for me in this school, at least not until he proves himself. And I am not going to let anyone get to me. I am going to start playing hard to get because that's what guys want, the chase, right?

Also, I hate school and I hate my life right now. I have no real friends at this high school, maybe just a few acquaintances. Lunch was horrible. I thought I had finally made a friend in chemistry, but when I went to go sit with her at lunch, she didn't even talk to me or introduce me while everyone else looked at me and wondered why I was even there. My brother looked on at me from the table of his popular friends, and I could recognize the face of pity. I couldn't take it anymore. I just want to have friends. Is that too much to ask? Why does everyone dislike me here? Oh God, hear my cry for help, and please help me find friends. I am not looking forward to another hellish day tomorrow. I am going to try and get some sleep, but maybe I will be lucky enough to not wake up at all. Goodnight.

*****

I was going into eighth grade when we moved to Pennsylvania. It was a tough time because I moved from the small town that I had grown up my whole life in and moved to a large town, whose middle school consisted of seventh, eighth, and ninth grades, so I would be coming right in the middle. I was dealing with the loss of my friends, my home, my town, and my brother not coming with us. I didn't have a specific identity when I moved here because my old town was so small we all knew each other in one sense or another, and there weren't really any cliques. This school had cliques. The popular kids came from the wealthiest of families, where the rest of us didn't. We certainly weren't poor here as my father had moved us because of a huge job promotion, but I also didn't know how to act like I wasn't one of the poorer families in town like I had been. I had no idea where I would fit in.

Over the next several years, I would go from group to group, trying to figure out where I belonged. It seemed once I felt comfortable in a group of friends, they would start bullying me, and I was forced to leave. Nor was it just guys this time, but I was desperate for approval from anyone. I was the new girl, and I found myself back to being the second child in my family, trying to compete with the golden child. It seemed like the harder I tried to fit in, the more I was rejected. It didn't help that I was a late-blooming tomboy, so where I once had a constant number of boyfriends from my old school, I now was being teased by the boys in middle school and high school as the girls my age already all had breasts and were more mature-looking. Back when instant messaging first came around, I would get cyber-bullied constantly by boys commenting on my flat chest or my long neck.

I was shy and new, and that combination did not bode well for me in a world where people fear the unknown. Kids would talk about me behind my back, but in a way that I could see they were talking about me. Someone wrote on my locker that I was gay, even though I had always been so boy crazy as far back as I could remember. The few friends I did make took my quietness as hostility sometimes and wrote nasty letters to me and handed them off to me in the hallway. Didn't they realize one of them made out with the boy I was dating while I was away one weekend and I needed time to sit and process that?

I spent a lot of time alone in my room. I was back to being a little girl again when no one would play with me. My imagination returned as I spent every night watching romantic comedy movies, but instead of believing I was an animal running through the woods, I was now fantasizing about the day I would have my perfect man and I could look back and laugh at all the people who were ever mean to me. These movies gave me something to look forward to in the future. They gave me hope that men were romantic, sweet, and one would sweep me off my feet someday, and we would live happily ever after. I drowned myself in these movies, which helped me in the moments of loneliness, but the next day was just a repeat of the same.

I ended up getting a job, working at the local movie theater when I was sixteen. It was a whole new start for me as I worked with a lot of people several years older than me, and they saw something different in me than the kids I went to high school with. I enjoyed the new attention and felt great about myself again. Luckily for me, there wasn't the greatest pool of female employees, so I got a lot of the attention and I morphed into an outgoing and flirty person. My confidence slowly started building as I enjoyed being the object of a lot of guys' eyes. Unfortunately, that's all I was to some of them, and one took it too far one day and slapped me really hard on my bottom. A manager got wind of the incident, but I was so scared about getting him in trouble and all the guys being mad at me that I begged the manager not to say anything, and I wasn't going to report it. I would forever be traumatized by the act of being slapped though.

I started hanging out with and developing crushes on some of the male managers and other employees who were all in their low to mid-twenties as I was by then sick of guys my age and found the older ones more mature and desirable. Matt was someone I had my eye on from the first day I started at the theater. He was tall, thin, and very handsome and had the bad-boy persona. He knew I had a crush on him for a long time and did not treat me great for several months, until one day, I got the nerve to seek him out and ask him why he hated me so much and why he treated me the way he did. I guess he was taken aback because after that, he started treating me a lot better. I continued pursuing him and started inviting him to group outings, and he eventually fell for me and we started dating. I was seventeen, and he was twenty-four. All of a sudden, I could care less about what people in high school thought about me. I had an older attractive boyfriend and a new group of friends that felt much better than the immature kids my age, and they gave me the validation I needed to feel like I fit in somewhere.

When I finally graduated high school, I decided I would morph into a new identity in college and leave my past traumas behind. I was excited to start over as a different person and leave my days of watching romantic comedies in my room alone every weekend behind. I walked into college orientation that day with a new story and a new body as I was finally hitting puberty. I bought new cute and sexy clothes and decided I was going to be a popular cheerleader. I played the part as best I could and made plenty of friends with what seemed to be the other popular kids from their high schools over those two days. I felt accepted again by peers my age and was excited to start college that fall.

Unfortunately, during freshman year, I shared a room and walls with all the really popular girls from high school, and they saw right through me. They were horrible, and my old shy self came back out. That year, I was bullied by my roommate and her friends as they started stealing my belongings and blasting their music while I was trying to sleep in bed. It got to a point where I moved anything that wasn't a necessity back home and anything that was a necessity, I locked up in a chest I held under my bed. One time, I accidently locked our door, not realizing she was in the shower; and as much as I apologized, she took it as war, and things got even worse. I could barely spend any time in my room and asked my boyfriend from back home to come visit me several days a week so we could sleep in the common room together on the couches so I didn't have to be in my own room. Instead of facing the bullying, I masked my pain and sought acceptance with others at school. Even though I had a boyfriend and I once could care less about what peers my age thought about me, I started indulging in the attention and affections of other guys around campus. They knew I was taken, but I flirted just enough to keep them interested in me, so I had that safety net at all times, knowing I was liked and wanted. As much as that felt great, my living conditions were so bad that I ended up moving back home the last three weeks of school to escape from my roommate and her awful friends.

In the following year, I ended up breaking up with Matt because it was an immature relationship filled with struggles with his friends and job, and I wanted something deeper and more long-term. I had no interest in dating around. I just wanted a serious relationship because I wanted to get married young, so I jumped right in to seeing Eric. Eric was ten years older than me and my district manager at work, so I think I was attracted to the taboo nature of it all. The first time I met him, I walked away and told my coworker, "*That* is our district manager? I can totally beat him up!" But he was very nice and personable, not like the one you would expect in that position. One night, I was in charge of walking over to the pizza place next door to pick up dinner for everyone, and Eric came with me. I got butterflies as we sat and talked for a bit. I couldn't believe a district manager was talking to me. I thought of him almost like a celebrity. He started joining in when we went on group outings to eat or midnight bowling, just like me and Matt's relationship had started. Eventually, we started dating in secret since it was not allowed within the company. It went on for several months until someone got wind, and I was forced to move districts. At least at that point, we could date in the open.

Since he was older, I knew he wanted to settle down and have a serious relationship, which was hard to find among guys my age. I was done looking for acceptance and approval from fellow students and friends, and I needed the consistent love of a serious relationship and marriage. He was kind, funny, caring, had a great job, and fun.

The physical attraction was not quite there for me, but his person-ality and status made up for that. He was Jewish, which I had never dated before, so something about the appeal of that unknown was there for me as well. I figured we all had the same God, so who cares? Even though he was small and goofy, I still felt special because he liked me. I fell in love with him one weekend away down in Florida, visiting his friends and watching him karaoke to Michael Jackson. Seeing a man out of his element but seemingly being so much in it is a strong quality of attraction for me.

Three weeks prior to graduation, he asked me to marry him. It was one thirty in the morning, and I had been asleep in bed after a long day volunteering for Habitat for Humanity and helping build a house. It was not the romantic proposal I had always dreamed about that they did in the movies I drowned myself in. It didn't even seem serious. His sister was asleep in the next room; we had just had a full day and plenty of opportunities to do it, why was he waiting until I was not even fully conscious? After telling him no about three times in a confused fog as to why it was happening then, I finally agreed. I reluctantly made love to him that night and tried to go back to sleep. The next day, I got up early and went to the gym to be alone. I wasn't quite ready to face his sister or anyone else at that point, and I wasn't sure why. I had a wide range of emotions in my head, but I couldn't pinpoint any particular one. I just knew I wasn't as excited as I prob-ably should have been.

CHAPTER 3

The Father

August 4, 2007

I don't know what to do anymore. My counselor is the only one who knows, and she's not providing me with any of the answers I am looking for. Who else can I turn to? I have never been so confused in my life. Things with Dad are worse than ever. He wants to bring her to the wedding. I can't even write her name. Why? Why would a person like that, who did that, want to show her face at an event she has already ruined by entering our lives? Why would he want to do that to us? To me? Hasn't enough damage already been caused? I am supposed to be getting married in a month, and I can't focus on that. I don't even know if I am doing the right thing at this point. Is the same thing going to happen to me? Am I ready for this? We got into another screaming match over the phone today about her. He told me he was taking me out of his will. Ha. Was that supposed to get me to cooperate and want a relationship with him? That was his ammo? Did he even know me at all? Like I cared about money. That just goes to show how unemotionally connected we've been and how little he knows of his own daughter. That's all he could ever talk to me about—school, money, the car, and work. We didn't know each other at all. He thought by threatening me with being taken out of the will, I would somehow magically accept this woman as some sort of stepmother at my wedding. I don't know. I am lost. I am not even excited about this wedding or marriage at this point. All that I knew about it was fake. Everyone acts cordially when they are really miserable inside. They let it build up until one day, something like this happens and families are shattered. Help me, God?

*****

It was Good Friday, 2006. I had gotten engaged the week before and would be graduating college in a couple of weeks. I went home that afternoon to a silent household. My father was sitting in the living room on the couch, awkwardly, with a present on the coffee table. It wasn't my birthday, so I was confused, but I sat down next to him. I could tell something wasn't right, and a knot in my stomach started forming. The next hour was a blur. Everything I had come to know about life was ripped out of my chest as my father revealed he had had an affair and would be leaving us after twenty-five years of marriage to my mother. My father? He was quiet and shy and just a normal guy who provided for his family, and he did what?

I gasped for air as it felt as though I was being choked, and tears quickly welled up in my eyes. I couldn't quite process all that he was telling me. I heard excuses. He had so many opportunities over the years on business trips, women throwing themselves at him. He was good then; he should be commended for lasting as long as he did. Was I supposed to be happy he didn't already have several affairs prior? Was he telling me that's how men were? Should I expect that in my future husband I just got engaged to? Was there an apology in there? Did he take any responsibility? I heard him say things about my mom. Negative things. Something about how she wasn't giving him what he needed, and he was a man, and men have needs. There were certain things men needed to sustain in a marriage. But he got me a present. Perfume. That was somehow supposed to make up for what he was doing?

He said he was going to live at our family vacation home in Vermont—the one we built together from the ground up fifteen years prior. So many great memories there. Weekend trips in the winter skiing, Thanksgivings, Christmases, summer getaways, fishing and boating in the nearby lakes. He met her up there. He was going to check on the house after a power outage one weekend, and when it was back on, instead of coming back home, he went to the bar and met her. She was going to be living with him in our house. The house was tainted, ruined, and soiled.

He told me goodbye as he stood up and walked out of the house. I stood up against the living-room window with tears rolling down my face in disbelief at the information I just had to take in. I looked out, desperately thinking this was all a dream as he drove off in his blue BMW sports car. A weight lifted off his shoulders—free from his past life, his family, his wife, music blasting, and excited to get up to Vermont to see her. As he drove out of sight, I fell to the floor. I lay facedown, screaming and sobbing all at once, thinking we were a normal family, and this couldn't be happening right now. I was alone. Abandoned. Everything I had ever believed in was suddenly a lie.

A little while later, I heard my mom come rushing in, frantically shouting my name, "Ellie! Ellie!" I couldn't pick myself up off the floor to even respond to her, but she found me and threw her arms around me. She had gotten the news about six days prior. My brothers got it three days prior. I was the last to find out. I would not know what it felt like for a mother to try and comfort her child in the midst of her own heartbreak until many years later. She was stronger than I ever could have imagined. All we could do was hug each other and cry. She had been there waiting in a parking lot outside of the neighborhood for him to drive away. What she had to have been going through knowing her husband was at their house, breaking her daughter's heart as he revealed the same thing to her as he had done to her a few days prior.

Good Friday became engrained in my mind as "Bad Friday." I had experienced a death and a loss in my family, except there would be no resurrection with this one. It was over. My family was broken. Ron came over shortly after, and a couple hours later, Evan called and said he was able to get a last-minute flight up here for the weekend. It's amazing how it takes a devastating circumstance for a family to come together. I can see that now, but it was the last time all of us would be staying over together at that home as a family. We didn't really know what to do that weekend. Normally, it would have been amazing, fun, and full of laughter—like it had been in times before. We would have stayed up late playing board games and talking about childhood memories. Instead, we sat there unsure of what to even say or think about what our father had just done and the man he had become. Maybe we really didn't even know him at all our whole lives. We were mostly speechless.

After making it through that first weekend and my brothers returning back home, I was left with having to face my last two weeks of senior year of college not knowing how to even function. I had been the lead on each of the projects in all my business classes but had to tell my group members that I could not finish out fully. Luckily, I had been on top of everything, so they didn't have to do too much more, but I didn't even care. I had the support of my sorority sisters, but every time I tried to talk about it, I would start crying. Eric didn't know what to do because his parents were still together. They were happy. Intact. Whole. I was now part of a broken family.

I could not even enjoy my engagement because I no longer believed in marriage. What was supposed to be a joyous time in my life quickly turned into a nightmare filled with every negative emotion imaginable. My brothers and I were quickly pulled into the trenches. As if seeing your mother go through all the emotions of learning about an affair then having her husband leave her wasn't bad enough, my father started pointing the blame at us, and every conversation turned into an all-out screaming fest. Not only had we physically lost our father as he went off to live in Vermont with the mistress, but emotionally as well. He must have had it in his head that he could live in an open marriage and stay with this woman, but when my mother filed for divorce, his hostility toward her filtered through on us. You would think divorce would be easier when kids are older, but there is never a good time. It is a brokenness that can't ever be reglued.

Going through this period of trauma took its toll on me as well as my relationship with my fiancé. Seeing two people after twenty-five years of marriage suddenly despise each other was unheard of to me. Everything I thought was normal and fine throughout my entire childhood was brought up as reasons my dad did what he did and why their union was dissolving. Were the problems I was having in my own relationship not normal then? Was I destined for the same path? I no longer had any guidance, and I felt like I had no one to turn to.

I struggled a lot over the next year and a half and found myself in counseling because apparently, I had more problems than I thought. Issues I thought were normal in a relationship, I started seeing as a red flag. Even though I disagreed with everything my dad did and the way in which he went about it, I didn't want to admit that on some level I understood some of what he was saying. I brought these concerns up to my counselor, but when our sessions came to an end, I decided to go through with the wedding, which brings us to September 7, 2007.

Issues were still unresolved between my father and the rest of us. We had agreed after several fights, he would not be bringing "her" to my wedding. On September 7, 2007, I had just come down after getting ready for my rehearsal dinner with a huge glow strewn across my face. My oldest brother Evan had just come over, nervously pacing back and forth, head fixated on the ground as if he was keeping something enormous inside.

"Dad is bringing Denise to the wedding!" he suddenly blurted out. "She came into town with him, and she plans to crash the wedding." The smile quickly turned into a horrid expression. I felt my knees got weak, and I lost my footing. My mom's jaw dropped, and she too had to grab hold of the counter to keep her footing. I had no intentions of drinking that night, but my mom immediately poured a glass for me and an even bigger one for herself.

I would say that was the first night I started drinking heavily. After an entire bottle of wine later, downed so fast I could barely taste it, I was ready to face all one hundred of my rehearsal dinner guests with this enormous weight on my shoulders dragging me down. I entered the room drunk, out of my mind, in front of a hundred people, most of whom consisted of my in-laws' friends and all out-of-town guests, which were all my fiancé's friends. My bridesmaids quickly took hold of me and walked me through the room, getting me through the introductions. I looked over and saw my father approaching me and clenched the hand of my dearest friend next to me.

Even though he was kind enough to leave her out of the rehearsal dinner, he would not give into my pleadings to keep her home the next day. "You promised me she wouldn't be attending," I begged. He also promised to stay with my mother until death did them part. A lot of good promises did. What good is a promise if one cannot keep it? There was no convincing him. I prayed that night for a miracle as I was tucked into my childhood bed, uncertain what the next day would bring.

I woke up the next morning with a positive attitude and went about my day. I thought there was no way a home-wrecker would have the guts to show up to a wedding of the child of the man she had an affair with. There was no way, and I prayed about it. As we were hanging out in the bridal suite, waiting for the ceremony to start, I started hearing yells. I walked out to see what was going on. Two of my bridesmaids yelled to another, "Get her back in that room!" Denise did show up at the wedding right before the ceremony, which is where my army of protectors had to jump in and deter her from entering the premises. I hadn't even met her yet, and she was trying to cause commotion on the most important day of my life.

Luckily, the army succeeded; and after a bit of yelling and profanity on part of my sisters-in-law, she finally retreated. Of course not without damage to all my family who had witnessed or had been a part of it, but luckily, the day was about me, and I will be forever grateful for those who took the brunt of everything to keep me out of the wind and in la-la land. My brothers walked me down the aisle, my dad sat by himself during the ceremony, then left shortly after, but I really didn't care anymore. The anxious anticipation was finally over, and I moved on with my day of celebration.

It would be years before we really started talking again and even more after that before I would ever get an apology. I couldn't see him without alcohol involved. It hurt too much. I went through a bottle of wine each dinner, each visit to his new apartment, and each visit from him to my house. It was the only thing to numb my emotions and get to a point where I could tolerate what he did and the lies he would tell me. I learned I couldn't trust my father anymore, and he no longer was a necessity or someone I could look up to in my life. I turned to my new husband to fulfill that role at that point.

CHAPTER 4

The Husband

March 31, 2016

Wow, it's been a really long time since I've written in here! So much has happened—marriage, kids, work, a business, life has happened. I am sitting here on my deck, overlooking this beautiful yard, living a very happy life. However, my marriage is not a happy one, and I do not know what to do. Seven weeks ago, Eric fell on the ski slopes, and it was the most scared I have ever been. I prayed that he would be all right and he was, just with a broken hip after all that. Despite it being a huge responsibility for me to take care of him, the kids, the dogs, the house, and the business, I was actually kind of excited to have him around more and hoped we could have more fun together. Everything happens for a reason. I originally thought this was to make our marriage stronger. However, I fear it may have had the opposite effect.

What has bothered me about Eric over the last few years has only been exacerbated now, and I am not sure whether to feel guilty or justified or just plain sad. He is a hard worker and a handyman. He is good at his jobs and will most likely do any of the "manly" jobs around the house or the business. With that, I don't think he is a great husband or father, or at least the kind I think we deserve. I feel like his priorities are sleep, computer, and television. I understand in the beginning I had to do everything, but once he was well enough, he should have started helping me more with getting up with the kids and putting them to bed at night. It's like the last thing he feels like doing is tucking them in at night and that's not how it should be, especially now that he isn't working or doing much of anything during the day. *I am exhausted too! Raising young kids is tough work, but we should share in the responsibilities, especially when I am working full time raising our other baby, the business.*

How he talks to me is unacceptable. I am repulsed by him sexually. What attraction I used to have is gone after comment, after degrading comment. Once we become mothers, things that are attractive are respect, equality, helping out around the house, being a great father, and wanting to play with the kids, and maybe trying to keep up with your appearance once in a while. He gets a kick out of taunting me with how he doesn't care about letting his looks go and doesn't try for me anymore.

He has become boring. This is a big one for me. The whole reason I fell in love with him was because he was outgoing, had a lot of friends, was great in social situations, and was always up for doing things. I no longer think his jokes are funny and, instead, regard them as perverse. He doesn't have any friends that I know of, and where he didn't want to go out with me anymore, now he does, but I no longer want him to. He also never wants to go anywhere or do anything with the kids. I have to come up with everything, and that's mostly okay, but he gives me a hard time about it because he just wants to sleep and doesn't have the energy. He keeps saying how old he is but I am not, and he doesn't even try to compromise.

Lately I have been enjoying just hanging out with friends at night. I never had so many friends before. I absolutely love that I have become this new social butterfly, and I am getting so much attention now that I have never had before, and I almost love the double life. I enjoy hanging out by myself with people, rather than as a couple. For so many years, I had to fill the emptiness I've felt with him working nights and never wanting to do anything with me with making new friends; and where I once longed for the nights he was home, I now was longing for the nights he went to work. I knew I

wouldn't be bothered to have sex those nights and found my fulfillment in the company of other mothers and a lot of wine. I recognize
my part in not wanting to have sex with him, and it's not really fair
for him. I recognize his comments and attempts are out of desperation for not being fulfilled in that area. I cannot help how horrible I
feel when he says them though.

I don't know. It's nothing horrible. He is a good guy as others
know him, but should I be feeling like this? Will it be like this for the
next forty-plus years? Won't I go crazy? Right now I have my friends
to distract me and talk me through it, but will I always? What then?
When we don't have the kids and he's retired, what the heck do we
do then? Is it better to separate now and devote our energy into being
friends, coparents, and business partners? We will have to see.

*****

I sat there on the far side of the couch, right leg crossed over
the left, hand holding up my head, and my eyes focused intently on
the same spot on the floor I had been looking at for the last forty
minutes. I half-listened as my husband and the counselor discussed
whatever issue we were up to, the other half trying to think about
what my next step would be. I felt sad, but there were no tears coming down. I had cried enough, I had decided. It was his turn now.

Ten years prior, on September 8, 2007, it was the happiest day
of my life. I woke up that morning without a care in the world. I had
a smile stretched across my face, thinking about how at the end of the
day, I would be a married woman. Still slightly hungover from the
night before and the drama of my father, I grabbed a bag of frozen
peas, put it over my eyes, and sat out on the deck with my family and
reminisced of childhood memories and what good the day would
bring for future memories. I took my dog for a walk for a little peace
and reflection, waited for my limo to arrive, and soon joined the rest
of my bridesmaids to get our hair and makeup done.

It was a joyous day. Besides the brief anxiety attack I had after
the mistress showed up, I had a smile on my face from start to finish. Even though it had been a rough year up until then, right up

until the night before with the whirlwind of emotions and abundance of drama from my dad coming into town, I was ready to put it all behind me and live in the moment. I had no more anxiety about marriage that day and felt ready to be a wife and excited for Eric and I to begin our new lives together.

After the ceremony, I was excited to start drinking and eating, taking pictures, mingling with friends and family, and, of course, dance! Everything was imperfectly perfect, and I was on cloud nine because I had just married my best friend. The night for me was about having fun in the company of friends and family. Unfortunately, that mindset had a large part in what brought us back to this point in my life because it should have been about something else, something so much more, and I had no idea at that time being just twenty-two years old.

We were on our way home from the counseling session, and Eric asked me what was going through my mind. I was thinking back to our wedding day, and a flashback of the last ten years invaded my mind. We had been through so much together—job losses, demotions, health scares, opening our own business, home and building purchases—the list was endless. We had two wonderful children together, Kayla first in 2010, just four days after getting the keys to our new business. Greg came next in 2012, but we had found out in utero that he was going to be born without part of his brain, which would make him a special-needs child. It was endless tests, doctors, therapists, and questions with him over the years as he was developmentally delayed and would be nonverbal. We were strong for the life we had created, and he really was my best friend. At that point though, that was all that I felt for him. "I just don't know if I believe in marriage anymore. There's no point. People treat each other differently, attraction goes away, and then spouse's cheat." Three months prior to this day, our lives were changed forever.

Eric and I took Kayla and Greg, and we headed up to the mountains for a long weekend trip with some of our friends and their children in February. We rented a house where all of us could stay, and we planned to ski for two days with the kids in ski school. Our family made it up there first, and after we put the kids to bed, Eric and I were able to relax and talk with a nice bottle of wine. It was so relaxing because there was no cable and almost no reception, so we were forced to be away from any technology that normally consumed us on an everyday basis. For a moment, it was just nice to be together, alone. Wine had a way of loosening me up and letting go of any negative feelings, seeing him in a different way, and just enjoying that exact moment. Anytime Eric and I were on any kind of date, I needed wine to turn into the wife I knew I should be. I needed it to numb my emotions and tolerate the situation better just as I did with my father. I don't think Eric cared, because for a few hours, he had the fun and flirty girl he met twelve years ago, just like my dad would have his old girl back.

The other guests began arriving shortly after, and we prepared for what we expected to be a wonderful weekend filled with laughter, games, catch-up talk, and skiing. We enjoyed the rest of our night all together laughing, drinking, playing games, then headed to bed in preparation for skiing in the morning and the -27 degrees it was supposed to be that day on the mountain.

I had been skiing since I was three years old, so I was pretty comfortable on the slopes. Eric had only learned a few years ago because it was something I enjoyed doing and wanted him to be part of it. He had a couple of lessons, but between work and children, we just didn't get to the mountains enough to keep up with any sort of consistent practice. We had been skiing only for about an hour when I stopped to wait for him, and as I looked back, I saw he had fallen again. I remembered being frustrated because he fell a number of times and he was taking a long time to get up. *What a selfish feeling*, I thought.

After a few minutes, I looked back up the mountain and saw a man approached him and talked to him, but I couldn't really see what was going on as he was a good fifty yards back up the mountain from where I was. My heart started pounding suddenly as I saw the man take off his own skis to put up as a barrier then start checking Eric's neck and back area. Thoughts raced through my mind as I imagined him being paralyzed and what we would do.

Even though it was fifty yards away up a steep mountain, I climbed as fast as I could, almost fainting myself from how worked up I was from both the climb and how hysterical I was thinking my husband could be seriously injured. The medics started swarming around him at that point, and when I finally approached, there were at least fifteen people around him trying to help. Eric screamed as they tried to move his leg, and as he did, I started blacking out myself and had to sit down.

He would have a broken femur bone. We would know this after an excruciating ride down the mountain on the back of a board being dragged by a ski patrol worker, a forty-five-minute ride via ambulance to the closest hospital, then finally an X-ray after a few hours in the hospital room. He would have surgery that night, which involved putting a metal rod in from his hip to his knee, and it would be a nine to twelve months full recovery period.

At first, all I could think about was how we were going to manage our jobs and getting the children to and from school and appointments. Then it was waiting on him 24-7, all while keeping up with the rest of the household. But my final thought was *Thank God I won't have to have sex with him for a while.* Unsure of where that thought came from, I quickly pushed it to the back of my mind and thanked God he was alive.

The weeks that ensued were extremely difficult for all parties involved. He literally could not do anything, and I had to be there for him 24-7 to assist him with everything from bathing to helping him go to the bathroom. Besides waiting on him throughout the day, I also had to take over all the childcare and household duties, all while trying to run my business as best as I could without also being there throughout the day. I know he was in the worst pain out of all of us physically, but I took the biggest toll mentally.

As the pain began to lessen for him and he started gaining more movement in his leg, he depended on me less and less for things and finally was able to go to the bathroom himself and get up to get his own food or drink. I finally was able to go to work for longer stretches now since he could do those basics, so it began to get a little easier for all of us, but I was still running around all day long getting the kids to and from school and activities, working, keeping up with household chores, and getting everyone fed, bathed, and to bed. I was exhausted each night, and once I got the kids to bed, I crawled right into mine and conked out.

One night, he was lying in bed watching television, and I was just about finished with another exhausting day, getting into my pajamas, when he said something to me that would change our lives forever. He made an extremely disrespectful sexual comment to me as I was standing there, completely disheveled and weathered from another hard day's work.

"Are you serious?" I said exasperatedly. "I have been waiting on everyone in this house hand and foot day in and day out for the last few weeks, and you want me to do that for you right now? You have a broken femur for crying out loud! You can hardly piss on your own, let alone do anything sexual!"

"Just because I have a broken femur doesn't mean you can't give me pleasure." I was so disgusted by my husband in that moment I stormed out the door and slept in the guest room that night. He had been disrespectful to me when it came to sex for the last few years, and it was a huge problem for us. But never before did I feel so revolted, so used, and so uncomfortable in my body, like I was meant to be some sort of sex slave to him.

One day, I came home and he was fixing our wooden gate on the deck. I was a little taken aback he was able to do something like that but was happy he was getting better. When it came time for the nighttime routines of dinner, bathing the children, and getting them to bed however, he remained plopped on the couch and in front of the television. When I asked him for help, he said he couldn't because he was still recovering, yet he felt good enough to fix gates and receive sexual pleasure. My frustrations grew as I realized I had married someone who wanted a servant as a wife, and that simply was not me.

As I was thinking about September 8, 2007, in that car ride back after our counseling session, instead of remembering how it was the best day of my life like I had always thought, my mind shifted to focusing on that night in the bedroom. It wasn't out of character for him to ask that of me when I wasn't up for it. We had long struggled with sexual intimacy. Sex was never anything I enjoyed. It felt more like a duty than a privilege or a pleasure, a task in the day that needed to be checked off to keep the man happy so he wouldn't stray. I always needed to be drinking to get me through it. After all, I did not want to end up like my mother, abandoned and alone after her husband strayed, so I did what I could. I guess the shock of the circumstances woke me up more than anything.

I started thinking about the past. Counseling brought up these issues. Our therapist forced us to look at our entire relationship from the very beginning instead of what was happening right then. Memories started coming up of inappropriate and perverse talk, grabbing me at inappropriate times when I had repeatedly asked him not to and constantly making me feel guilty if I wasn't in the mood or was too tired. Being a breastfeeding mother of two young children, running a business and working seven days a week left little time for excess energy. It was a tough time period for me, and there was no patience on his end. We ended up having sex in the shower a lot because it killed two birds with one stone for me, and it was quick and clean and did the trick. There was nothing in it for me except for him to not ask me for it the rest of the day.

It got to a point where I proposed we would do it once a week on a certain day if he would not talk perversely, touch me inappropri- ately, or not try to guilt me into it the rest of the week. Eventually, I could not even hold up my end of the bargain sometimes if I had my period or was too tired, and he complained and we fought over it. I knew this was not a way to live for a woman of only thirty years old. I should want to have sex with my husband, right? He had every right to complain and grab me whenever he wanted, right? These thoughts all led to the moment when I told him at dinner that we need to start counseling because I felt like I was done and I didn't know what to do anymore.

Two therapists and many months later, we decided to separate. It was the most difficult decision I have ever had to make, but I could no longer live my life knowing he deserved more than what I could give him and not knowing what I wanted or who I even was for that matter. I realized over the last several years, I was looking to other things to bring me happiness and fulfill a hole I had inside of me. I filled that hole with friends, alcohol, fantasies of other men, money, home improvements, and vacations. Things that were great in making me happy in the moment but left me wanting more in the long run. Just prior to going to the mountains, we had a realtor and were looking at buying a beach house. It was the only thing I could say was exciting in my life at that time, and I figured if we could acquire a beach house, that would make all our problems go away, and I would be happy. We were actually going to bid on one right upon our return from the trip until something intervened. It wouldn't have helped. Each time I tried filling my hole with one of these idols, I still was left empty and in search of the next best thing. So instead I decided to open up that hole further in search for someone else to come and fill it.

The weight that was lifted, knowing I was no longer his servant, was enormous, and I felt like I gained a little part of me back that day and was ready to tackle what lay ahead for me. The separation would last a few years, most of which we lived in the same home. This would make meeting anyone tricky, but I if I was going to be without a husband, I know I needed to meet someone else so I wouldn't be alone. I had no idea the next few years would feel like a reality show of dating escapades resulting in the most dramatic, unexpected conclusion of them all.

CHAPTER 5

Entering the Dating Game

September 5, 2017

My Ideal Romantic Partner

One of the most important things to me would be to feel a strong desire for that person. I want to be attracted to them in every sort of way. Physically: tall and skinny, handsome face, good hygiene, dresses nice, and smells good. Emotionally: genuinely enjoys spending time with them, having deep and meaningful conversations. Sexually: having a strong desire to kiss and be sexual with them, getting excited at the thought of having them, being able to kiss and touch without it always having to lead to sex—wanting all parts of their body and having it feel good.

They would do something for work that I admire or look up to or find desirable in them—like a musician, athlete, a position involving kids, like a teacher, coach, trainer, or anything unique and exciting—not only for me to be interested in, but knowing they love their job and are fulfilled with it.

There has to be passion there on both ends or "chemistry." Missing the person so much when they are away then being so excited upon their return. Having such a deep connection with that person and wanting to learn and explore new things about them each day and having them want to know as much as they can about you, not being able to imagine life without them and doing anything you can to hold onto them.

I want someone who shares passion for my favorite things, like theme parks, video and board games, being outside, sports, relaxation, traveling, the beach, water, boats, biking, hiking, etc. I also want them to introduce me to activities they are passionate about so I can try new things and have them want to try my things. I want someone who comes up with fun and unique date ideas, picks places so I don't always have to think about it.

Personality-wise, they have to be fun, energetic, happy, funny, see the positive in things and not be down or negative all the time. I want someone who can keep up with my level of energy and motivate me to do things that are good for me, like healthy cooking and eating, exercise, socializing, trying new things, etc. He can't be afraid to be the domineering one sometimes, giving me pushback if I am being unreasonable. Taking charge in situations and standing up for me and his family.

He needs to be social and hold his own in a group setting, being able to talk to anyone. Communication between each other is also a necessity as I want to be able to tell him everything.

Lastly, he is extremely affectionate and is not afraid to hold hands, kiss in public, buy me little surprise gifts, write me little notes, give back rubs, and do any kind of romantic gestures to keep the romance alive.

The One-Night Stand

Being on the market again felt a little strange. After all, I had been attached to someone since I was seventeen years old. The last couple of years in my marriage had been pretty miserable, and I remember going out with friends and almost wishing I wasn't married as different men would approach me throughout the evenings. I was always faithful, but was now really my time to go out, meet people, and go on dates? This was something I never was able to do because of my choices to commit so early on in my life. I was hesitant, ill-prepared, yet excited about my potential opportunities and began to wonder if this was really my chance to get that ideal romantic partner I needed to write about during one of our couple's counseling sessions just several months prior. I developed a "bucket list" in my head about different men that I wanted to meet. Looking back, it was a sick game I was entering into, but I had been let down, abandoned, or teased by guys growing up, so this was my time to make up for it and prove how attractive I really was. I wanted to somehow get back at everyone who hurt me and say, "Look at me now." There was only *one* who would be really looking.

Jake was the first one on my bucket list. I didn't know of him, but he would soon become my first conquest: the one-night stand. After fourteen years in a committed relationship, I went to opposite end of extremes. The idea of sleeping with someone the first night I met them had always been such a turn off for me, but I was ready to try it out and see what it was like. This was finally my time to explore what the dating world was all about and had to offer.

Going into the night, I had no intentions of making this conquest of course. I didn't say to myself as I was putting my dress and makeup on that night, "I am going to have sex with a complete stranger and never talk to them again." I wasn't trying to be a predator or prey that night. I was simply accompanying my friend Amy on one of her dating website dates in Northeast Philadelphia—a place I was pretty unfamiliar with. We met her date at his house, along with two of his roommates. It was definitely a little sketchy of a scenario, and I was pretty uneasy being in a stranger's house with two other men I didn't know, so I was happy when we went out to a restaurant and sat at the bar instead.

He was not my typical type, if I even had one at that point. It had been so long, and I hadn't really been thinking about my ideal type at all; but at first glance, the attraction wasn't necessarily there. He was short and a little goofy looking, but he was sweet and funny.

Come to think about it, he was an even shorter version of my ex-husband, so maybe it makes sense that he would be the first guy I would encounter after the separation. The conversation was there, and I quickly became comfortable with him and the situation. He bought me some drinks, so that certainly helped loosen up the mood of hanging out with complete strangers.

After a couple hours, we all headed back to their house. Amy left me alone with him as she escaped to have some one-on-one time with her date. I was a little frustrated she left me as I really had no interest in this guy, but it wasn't unlike her to leave me in uncomfortable situations like that while she pursued what she wanted.

He poured me another drink as we awkwardly sat on the couch while the others had all dispersed. Soon enough, we started kissing, and he was touching me all over. I didn't really know how one thing led to another, but pretty soon, I was in the upstairs bathroom with my dress hiked up, my underwear on the floor, and him behind me. I was facing the mirror but couldn't even look at myself as I didn't want to watch with shame how I allowed a complete stranger I had just met invade my body.

Well, I got it over with. Having sex with a complete stranger after being with someone for the last twelve years. It was not all it was cracked up to be, but somehow, I wanted more, just not with him. I couldn't even look at him afterward and quickly told him goodbye. He pursued me for a few weeks after that, but I just gave him the runaround. I felt so much shame afterward I couldn't even look at him in the eyes again and had no interest in feeling that way again. It was time to see if the next one could bring any better feelings to me.

The Bad Boy Bartender

Toward the end of my marriage, I spent a lot of time out with friends at a local restaurant and bar and made friends with a lot of the regulars and bartenders. There was one bartender in particular I thought was devilishly handsome, and of course as part of their jobs, bartenders probably have to be flirtatious to those of the opposite sex because, naturally, they want people to order more drinks and tip greater amounts. I bought into it of course and started going on nights Brian was working to see him. He knew I had a crush on him as I am pretty open about my feelings and desires, but I could never really tell if he was interested or not. He kept me guessing and vying for his attention, because at that point, my self-worth relied on the likes of a cute bartender who slept all day and smoked marijuana in his free time outside of work. He made a delicious grape martini though and had a sexiness about him having the status of a bartender with drunk girls batting their eyes at him, so I thought if I was the one who could get to him over anyone else, then I would be special.

After months of coming to the restaurant and a lot of money spent trying to get his attention, I learned he was fired. I was upset I wouldn't see him again, but it turned out he played poker at the casino Amy played at and was friends with one of the guys she was seeing at the time. The four of us hung out one time, and at that point, we exchanged numbers, but it never really went anywhere after that. I remember it being a snowy night and the guys wanted us to come back to their house, but I had to get home because the roads were getting really bad. I was so excited to hang out with him but disappointed that it ended with that missed opportunity. *Should I have gone back to his house that night against my better judgment?* I thought to myself. And if so, would he still be talking to me? I was so upset with myself I didn't go along with his wishes that night. I tried texting him a couple of times after, but he was pretty impolite back to me and did not seem interested in me anymore. I kept going back to that night though, remembering how flirty he had been and thought there was no way he couldn't be interested in me.

About a month or two later, I received a text message from him out of the blue, asking to meet up at the casino. Excitement poured back into me as I thought maybe this could be my chance at a do-over. I had to have him and would do whatever it took to win over his approval of me. He came with a friend to the casino and showed up in a blue button-down shirt with gray pants and dress shoes. A vast difference from the restaurant T-shirt and pants I saw him in every time at work. I thought it was so cute; he looked like he had dressed up for me and still was in shock he was actually there for me. Once he got there, the friend left, and I ended up driving him back to his apartment. Once we got back there, he pulled out a bottle of red wine, and we talked for a while on the coach. Several glasses later, he took me into the bedroom, kissed me, and before I knew it, we were having sex.

I don't remember much except his body was out of shape and sweaty. I guess I had overlooked that with his handsome face and charming personality. It was taking a really long time, and I was ready for it to be over. When it was finally time for him to finish up, I have to say, I was relieved. There was nothing that actually satisfied me about it, except the fact that I had finally slept with Brian and I felt good about myself in that moment. I gathered my clothes and belongings and went home.

When I didn't hear from him at all that week, I texted him, asking if he wanted to go out, and he was pretty cold back to me. I was not sure exactly what I said, but in some pathetic way, I must have convinced him to let me come over again. It wasn't good enough that I slept with him that once, but I was offended that he wasn't reaching out, trying to get together again, so I needed to go over again and prove how I could make him feel good—so good that he would want to keep hanging out with me. That night went similar to the first. I didn't enjoy having sex with him, and I couldn't wait for it to be over; but at the same time, I felt like I needed it to somehow make him like me.

I went over there three times in total when I finally noticed something around his ankle. I didn't know what it was at first until I thought about it, and it was an ankle monitor. I would later learn that he was on house arrest for three months, and he must have reached out to me and met me at that casino right before the sentencing started. He needed to line up women that would be willing to come over to his apartment so that he could still have sex, even though he wasn't allowed to leave. He reached out to me several times after that, but I just kept making excuses as to why I couldn't come over. As much as I knew he used me at that point, I still felt bad for him and didn't want to tell him I knew what was really going on because I didn't want him to get mad at me. If he could be so rude to me and use me for sex, why wasn't I able to tell him off and expose who he really was and what he was doing and how I wouldn't stand for it? Would it have helped? Why did I care so much about what this man, who clearly did not care about me, thought?

I took the attention for a while until it dwindled down. At that point, I told him I just wanted to be friends as a way to let him down easy, without having to deal with any crazy confrontation that would start a fight or lead him to never want to talk to me again. He reached out here and there, but once he realized I wasn't coming over anymore, I never heard from him again anyway. After Brian, I decided I would go out and actually look for someone I could actually go on dates with because the late-night meetups for the sole purpose of meaningless sex was not fulfilling me in any way; in fact, it was emptying me.

CHAPTER 6

The Long-Term Unattached Relationships

September 28, 2016

Reed. I can't stop thinking about him all the time. All I want in life right now is to hang out with him, but he's not asking that much anymore. He'll text me almost every day. Little things and random conversations, saying he misses me then calls me cute little names like "boo." He asks me why I don't reach out to him the next day after we hang out, but then when I do try and have conversations with him, he usually doesn't want to talk long. I have never been more confused in my life. He said he couldn't go past a certain point with me. *Has he reached it and won't go out with me at all? What do I do now? Should I be short with him or not respond to him at all? Would that make things better or worse?* I am not good at the games. I am great at playing board games, but not games of life, people's feelings, and getting guys.

*****

During this time period in my life, I used every opportunity I could to go out and find fulfillment. I would get a babysitter three or four nights a week to go out with friends so I could drink, party, and meet guys. I used my looks and outgoingness as a way to prove myself worthy, giving men whatever they wanted, even though I felt awful afterward. I felt like I was in a lose-lose situation constantly because if I didn't give myself to them, they may stop talking to me, and I would feel rejected; but if I did, I felt ashamed and guilty afterward. I constantly used alcohol as a way to bring out this confidence in myself when I went out and come off as fun and easy. Maybe I even used it as an excuse to do what I did so I wouldn't have to feel as ashamed after. "It was the alcohol that made me act that way and do what I did." I kept telling myself and others. They thought it was funny. My sexual adventures became the topic of conversation among gatherings with friends as they lived vicariously through me.

I never had this attention in middle school and high school before. Sure, once in a while, one of the "unpopular" boys may have taken an interest in me, but even if I "went out" with one of them, I still always got dumped eventually because of my own insecurities. But the rest bullied and teased me for being such a late-blooming tomboy. Boys would go out of their way to harass me even online about my flat chest and gawky figure. Now four chest sizes bigger and a full-grown woman, I was finally getting the attention I always desired back then, and I wanted to eat it up as much as possible as a way to get back at all those who were mean to me. I thought I felt happy and confident in myself, but I couldn't always shake the negative emotions that came with the burden of doing what I knew was wrong in the long run. I still wanted something more.

The Lead Singer

Only once before had a man caused me to stop midsentence, stealing my breath and my stare, and it took eight months for that other man to notice me back. Although Matt was the first man I was ever attracted to at first sight, it was a different kind of attraction since I was too young to understand what real chemistry was at the time. It was different with Reed. Different than anything else I had ever experienced. As my gaze followed him across the room, mouth half-opened from the word I hadn't finished in conversation, his eyes met mine, and a light flickered inside me.

I was sitting at the bar, chatting with Anna. We were what seemed like the only people under fifty in the venue as we anxiously awaited our favorite cover band to start playing. I had only met her a few months prior, but we bonded almost immediately over our relationship situations and love for live music. As we were having one of our hundred conversations about our separations, I began to say to her, "That's it. My next guy will be a singer or an actor! I need someone exciting!" As my thoughts and glare quickly shifted toward the other side of the room, I heard Anna say in the background, "Oh, that's the new lead singer of the band."

He was dark-skinned, with a gorgeous face, adorable hair, and a beautiful body. He had a smile so perfect it could melt your heart in an instant. "That's the new lead singer? Oh my god, he is beautiful. What was I just saying about wanting to date a singer?"

I tried to get back to our conversation, but I couldn't really keep my eyes off him. He was socializing with some of the people standing around by the stage as the band was getting set up, but I noticed him looking my way ever so often. I was now even more excited to see them perform than before, so we grabbed our drinks and headed to the front of the stage.

The first song he sang pretty much sealed the deal for me. I couldn't really pay too much attention to anything else going for-ward. They played for about an hour, then other bands came on, and they mingled with the rest of the crowd. I am not really sure what came over me because I have never done anything like this before, but I saw him standing at the bar, and I marched right over there and asked if I could buy him a drink. We talked on and off for the rest of the night, danced a bit, and it honestly was all quite a blur. I do remember sitting at the bar at one point, watching another band, and we were talking, and he leaned over to kiss me. That was the quickest I had ever met someone and then kissed them. That was not like me at all…but it felt great.

After that, we went for a walk. We walked through the town and sat on a bench and talked for a while. I felt an immediate connection with him, and it was amazing. I just wanted to keep kissing him. I couldn't stop. I knew Anna was back in the bar, completely by herself. I was so blinded I didn't even think about it. I really couldn't stop. He was so gorgeous and sweet. I noticed he had a tongue ring, just like Matt, which excited me more. Eventually, I had to get back to reality though. We exchanged numbers, and he walked me back inside so Anna and I could leave. As he walked me out for our final goodbye, it was almost impossible to break away from his lips. I didn't want our time to end that night.

He texted me that night, and we made plans already for the following week. It would be a whole week away, but I was so excited I could barely sleep. Throughout the week, he texted me sweet phrases, wished me good night, and always brightened my days. I didn't really know what to think at first. He was unlike anyone I had ever been with before. He was from a different world than me, and I wasn't really sure what his motives were. He seemed like a really genuine guy, but I was going through a lot in my life, so I tried to keep myself somewhat at a distance.

It wasn't too difficult to keep myself at that distance. He had a busy touring schedule, and I was swamped at my own job. I found it easy to get his texts and not respond to him for hours because I knew guys enjoy the chase. I was excited to see him again but terrified at the same time. This would be my first real date with someone whom I had only just met. All I could think about was telling him I was recently separated and that I had two kids. What would he think?

We decided to meet at a restaurant in a town in between our homes since we lived an hour apart. He arrived at the restaurant first, and I was trying to find it. I had gotten a little lost, so I called him, and he was trying to explain to me where to go, but I couldn't seem to find it anywhere. For one moment, I thought I was being pranked. This guy really wasn't at this restaurant and why wasn't I able to get to him? Then I remembered the moment I saw him in the distance. It was so far away, but I could see his figure as I walked toward the restaurant, and he was on the phone, with me, talking me through how to get to him.

He wore a black leather jacket and black jeans. He stood out so boldly on the white pavement in front of the restaurant, and I looked down toward the ground for a moment, trying desperately to hold back my smile. *This is really happening,* I thought to myself. I was moments away from being on a date with this beautiful specimen of a man. The night went great. Conversation flowed nicely, and we were very attracted to each other. We kissed at the end of the night again. I'm sure he wanted to go further, but that is all it got to. I was sure I wanted to, but for some reason, I was able to stop myself and called it a night. I was proud of myself.

The next few months, we went out several times, but distance and touring schedules made it difficult to see each other often. Each time we did get together, it did get a little harder to say goodbye because I fell a little harder for him. Each time I left, I regretted not saying more or being more myself because I was too caught up in trying to be perfect for him since he was like a celebrity to me. I thought as I fell harder, he fell back a little bit. He also started feeling the benefits of being the lead singer in a band and did not want to tie himself to one person. The more he pulled away, the more determined I was to get him back to where he was with me in the beginning. I was back to needing that full acceptance from him because if I wasn't good enough to be with him, then obviously, something was wrong with me.

Our time together went from hanging out and going on dates to me having to come to shows to see him. Sometimes, we would meet up after, and if I got a hotel room, he would stay over. I thought deep down he eventually just used me for a place to stay so he wouldn't have to drive home after a show at the beach, but I didn't have enough self-worth to stop it. I felt great that the lead singer was coming back with me; it didn't matter what time of the night it was or who he had been with prior to getting to me. This went on for the next couple of years and turned into late-night texts when I was feeling down about myself and I needed someone familiar to change that for me. There would be others in between, but it was comforting to always have someone familiar to fall back on.

The Guy from the Islands

All I remember of the first time I saw him was those piercing brown eyes with the darkest skin as he glared at me across the room during a routine reggae performance at a local restaurant in Jensen Beach. It was the first trip of what would be an annual tradition among my father, brothers, and me to visit his beach condo on Florida's west coast. My father wanted to take us to a local spot he usually hits to cater to my love of outdoor seating and live music.

The reason I don't remember much else is because I was unbelievably sick that weekend with strep throat, laryngitis, and a nasty cold. There was also the fact that I was married that first trip down, so I also wasn't exactly looking at people in that way when I was out. But something about him stuck with me because the following year, when I was so excited to come see the band perform again, I remembered him immediately and said to myself, "Ooh, the hot keyboard player! That's right!"

The trip this time occurred several weeks after Eric's accident. I was exhausted in every aspect of my life and needed the getaway. I arranged for Denise to fly up and help take care of both Eric and the kids while I flew down so I could enjoy another weekend with my dad and brothers. We did the same activities mostly, golfing during the day, then back to the pool for shuffleboard and cards in the evening. He also took us back to Joseph's to see the fun reggae band perform again.

We had such a fun first night that time. They played all our requests, and I got everyone up and dancing to the music. I couldn't keep my eyes off Tristan though. We locked gazes practically the whole time, all while I was showing off my fun personality with my goofy dance moves. He was the most gorgeous man I had ever seen. He was so ethnic and foreign to me, which was so sexy. His dark, dark skin with the whites of his eyes so bright against his face was so pleasing to my eye; he probably thought something was wrong with me, but I literally could not take my eyes off him.

After we left the restaurant that night, I came back to the condo and hopped on social media to look up the band and leave them a nice note to show them how much I liked their performance. I had hoped to get some information about Tristan (because at that point, I didn't even know his name), but not much was listed on there.

On the third night of our stay, I was able to convince everyone to come back to the restaurant after dinner so I could see them again and get in more time locking glares with this gorgeous man. I wasn't very subtle at all in my attempts to get him to notice me. I continued staring at him, as well as dancing right up in front of him with whomever was around. When they would take breaks, I made it a point to either go to the bathroom or get something at the bar in the other room since they sat at the tables in there away from the crowd.

At one point, my constant attention-seeking paid off. During one of my trips back from the bathroom, I heard someone calling my name in a soft, slow voice. I turned around, and to my surprise, it was coming from the table where the band was sitting, so I went over there and said hello. It was the first time I actually spoke with them, so I of course laid out the charm and the flirty laughter and asked them how they knew my name. They had seen my post on their social media page, so I was pleased to know my tactic had worked to get on their radar. I chatted with them for a few minutes, but sadly, the rest of my party were ready to leave, so I took one of their CDs and left them behind until the next year.

I could not get him out of my mind though. Since their names were listed on the CD I bought, I did some research and found his personal account on social media. Even though he lived in Florida, he was a lot older than I thought, and I knew next to nothing about him. I was disappointed to see he was in a relationship with someone already. I just couldn't get him out of my mind, with constant thoughts of his beautiful eyes staring into mine. I had always said that was one line I would never cross, but I figured it couldn't hurt to send a private message to their social media account to see if they would ever come to my area to perform. Within moments, I received a message back from one of the other members telling me to contact Tristan with questions about reservations.

I couldn't believe I had his phone number. Granted I probably would never be able to afford to book them for an event by me, I probably used it as an excuse to talk to him again. It took me a few days to work up my nerve, but eventually, I sent him a professional message, asking about bringing them to Philadelphia, and he sent back a message to call him anytime to discuss. I left it alone after that, knowing I would never have the guts to call him, but he remained in my thoughts as the most attractive man I had ever seen. I began the excitement of being able to see them again the following year. It would be a long time to wait, but what else was I supposed to do?

One separation and many relationship bucket-list items checked off later, I was finally in Jensen again with my dad. It was Thursday night before either of my brothers arrived and the first day of the week they would be playing. I was beyond excited. I thought about posting a message on their social media page, letting them know I was coming, but I opted not to since I figured they wouldn't remember me. It was so crowded when we arrived that my dad and I had to sit at the back-room bar for dinner and drinks. I couldn't even hear them play because of the distance, and I just became more and more anxious as I waited for us to finish and go in.

Luckily or unluckily, my dad took care of that for me as he started a fight in our seats, causing me to start crying and needing to rush to the bathroom to try and settle down. I had spent a lot of time getting ready to go out, and now, I was a blubbering mess. I fought back the tears and tried to go back and sit with my dad and start over the night, but the tears kept coming. I excused myself again and went over to the outside deck near where they were performing, and suddenly, the tears stopped, and a smile came over my face.

One of the singers looked at me from the next room over, and with a big smile and wave, he signaled for me to come inside. I could not even believe they remembered me, and from outside a window at that. I quickly forgot about my father in the other room, came to the front of the stage, and started dancing to their incredible music. I was at my happy place.

After they finished their first set, they all came over to say hi and give me hugs. I poured my heart out to them that I was their biggest fan and had been waiting all year to come see them. I was at about four martinis in at this point because of the uncomfortable state my dad left me in, but because of that, I finally had the nerve to strike up a conversation with Tristan. I told him how much I loved their covers of U2 hits, and he responded by saying how much he loved them and wanted to go to a concert. I said, "I have tickets to the show on June 18. You should come up and see them with me!" He agreed and even gave me his phone number and told me to text him that night to remind him of the date, and he would try to buy a ticket.

For the next couple of hours, he came over to talk with me during the breaks. I was usually with a group of new friends or people whom I had met the year before. Another martini in, and I even said to the group we were all with at one point, "I would be all over him, but he's married with a bunch of kids, so I can't do that." I guess the alcohol was really talking that night because I made several comments of the sort and kept putting my arm around him as we spoke.

The night came to an early end as they closed at ten thirty on Thursdays; so as my dad told me, it was time to go. I went over and gave everyone a hug goodbye.

"Make sure you text me that concert date so I can buy a ticket," he said.

"I definitely will as soon as I leave here," I replied. And with smile strewn across my face, I left that night happy and free of all the pain my dad had caused me early on.

For the next hour, after I got home, Tristan and I conversed back and forth via text message. For some reason, the conversation came so easy and natural, not like with Reed, whom I was still trying to get over. I would ask him a question about something, and he would respond not only with a reply but several, which made me feel so comfortable I just wanted to keep talking with him. I apologized for talking so long at one point, but he told me I was beautiful and I made the band's night. It was all the affirming I needed to hear after my father had tried to ruin my night for me.

The night didn't end there however. Apparently, neither of us was ready to say goodnight, and I found myself a little while later being picked up by him at my dad's complex and taking me out to play pool. He told me he was not married, but he did have six children, and he was significantly older than me; however, he didn't look a day over forty with his chiseled physique and perfect face. With an undeniable attraction toward each other, mixed with many martinis throughout the night, I soon found myself in a parking lot with him, letting him have my body in his car. This would happen one more night that weekend, and so started yet another long-distance non-committal "relationship" for me. I didn't care though. He was gorgeous, and I couldn't wait to show his picture off to my friends, who had been living vicarious through me because if I could get someone that attractive and also in a band, then I must be pretty enough.

Tristan and I remained in contact over the next couple of years, and even though we were many states apart, I loved getting the reassuring messages calling me "his queen" and so on and so forth. I knew it was mostly cheesy and used to get into my good graces to keep me on his hooks, but I could not deny the satisfaction I felt, knowing I had gotten this gorgeous man. Each time I went down to visit, I always showed up at the restaurant, and we would meet up. As satisfying as it was at first, I again felt something lacking. I knew I was probably being used, but I was still treated like a queen on the surface, so I didn't mind it. One day, I received a text from a woman who claimed to be his fiancé and started drilling me about our relationship. I asked him what it was all about, and he told me to lie to her. I knew then that I was now the other woman. I was Denise. I didn't know it, but it still didn't make me feel any better. They broke up shortly after, but I stepped back as I felt worse shame than ever before.

Even though there were a few long-term relationships in there, deep down I knew they weren't really relationships at all. Yes, we talked and texted outside of getting together over a couple of years, but they were really no better off than the late-night meetups with Brian. They cared a little more about me, but they still weren't trying to love me, like I deserved to be loved and enter into a real commitment. The feelings were there on my part, but I think I was more in love with the idea of these men than anything else.

CHAPTER 7

God Sends in a Messenger

January 27, 2018

Sadness. That's what I feel right now. I am in my sunroom with a glass of wine, playing depressing songs while tears are rolling down my face. It's only 3:00 p.m., but I don't care. I don't know what else to do. I am losing my friend. I feel abandoned again. Every time I get close, they leave. Why does God keep taking people away from me when I am happy? What am I supposed to learn from this? I do not understand. My tears are soaking the paper in my notebook. The ink is splotchy. I don't even know what else to write. I'm going to just go out tonight with Amy and Jessie and see about finding the next one.

The Personal Trainer

It's so cliché. Every woman who works out fantasizes about him. The tight shirts outlined every muscle in his upper body. The way he makes sweatpants and a hat look so sexy. When you do the exercise incorrectly so he has to put his hands on you to show you the correct way, but you can't help think about how all you really want them to do is rip your clothes off. When he sees you across the room and all of a sudden, you are motivated to work out just a little harder so he can see you really are athletic. The trainer. For me, he was the one that got away.

It was a couple years prior when I walked in to my high intensity interval training (HIIT) class, and I saw D standing in the corner, talking to a few people. I glanced over but quickly did a double take as I had never seen him before, and he was gorgeous. He was exactly my type: tall, dark, handsome, and very athletic looking. James, our normal instructor, came in and introduced D to the class as a new instructor at the gym and that he was going to be doing a ten-minute warm-up with us. I had placed my mat right up front that class as to be right near him.

I couldn't take my eyes off him. I didn't say hi of course, just continued to stare and hoped to catch his eye each time. From that point on, I was actually excited to go to the gym. I started coming more and more, taking note of what days and times he was there training and altered my schedule around that. Every time I walked in and caught a glimpse of him across the room, I got this feeling of giddiness and excitement and was motivated to work extra hard that time.

After a few months of staring at him each day, we finally started acknowledging each other and saying hello each time. One Thursday night, the gym management put on a member appreciation night with drinks and dancing, and he was there, so we actually spoke that night, and he learned my name and said he would friend me on Facebook. He was only twenty-five years old, a whole seven below me, but I didn't really care that much. A few more months went by of the weekly hellos, and each week, my desires grew stronger and stronger. I continued to live my life outside of the gym of course, going about dating the different guys on my "list" because I really knew nothing about this guy and if he even was with anyone.

One night I logged into my work Facebook account and saw his friend request in there from months ago, but I never used that account, so I was just seeing it then. I accepted and immediately mes-saged him, asking about personal training sessions. I knew I really didn't need them or could even afford an extra luxury like that, but I also didn't know how else to get to know him better. Two weeks later, I started my private training sessions.

I was so nervous during my consultation, but he made me feel comfortable. Obviously, as a trainer, you are working with people who are self-conscious about their bodies, so it is their job to make people feel comfortable, but he made me laugh, and I could tell there was more to him than just a gorgeous body and face. Training was difficult, but he made it fun. He asked a lot of questions about me and brought up a lot of unusual but interesting conversations. I always felt a little weird because I had this crush on him, and I am horrible at hiding things, so I felt like he knew it all along. So I would say dumb things, or be clumsy, but I didn't really care. I was actually excited about someone again and thought there was actually more substance to him than the guys I was used to. He also wasn't looking at me like an object, nor did he even seem interested in that, which could have been what drew me in further to him.

Training sessions were great, but it was time to pick things up a bit and put some feelers out for what his story was. He became the new object of my "drunk-texting" problem. I started out simple and professional, thanking him for making my body feel really sore. Then I started asking him to hang out with our group of friends from there. He never agreed; he just kept saying if one of the other trainer girls, his friend Catie, would go, then he would join. I could tell he was very shy, not like the extrovert I was, taking chances to meet new people, but that didn't stop me from continuing to try. During one of our training sessions one day, I did learn that he had a girlfriend, and I was extremely bummed.

I backed off from liking him but continued on with my last few sessions and continued being friends with him and trying to get him to hang out with us. Even though I couldn't have him romantically, I still really enjoyed his company and wanted to be friends because he was unlike other guys I knew. One summer day, I finally got him to come over when I was having a group of my gym friends over for dinner. He only stayed for a little bit, but it was definitely the start of a closer friendship. We had fun, and he agreed to come over again another time with just him and Catie.

The following week, they came over for dinner and then we went in the hot tub. I learned he had broken up with his girlfriend, so I suddenly had a romantic interest in him again. Not like it ever really went away, but I knew there wasn't a chance before, and now there was at least that possibility again. He always had a way of starting interesting conversation, so there was never a shortage of talking. He was genuinely interested in people's thoughts and opinions and getting to know them in as deep of a way as possible. The subject of my pending divorce came up each time we hung out from there on out, but I never could really talk about it fully.

I asked him to hang out a lot, but he never wanted to hang out one-on-one. It was confusing because I got the feeling that he enjoyed hanging out with me, but there always had to be at least one other person there. I didn't understand it because any guy I had spoken to before would have jumped at the chance to get me alone. Why did I enjoy this sort of rejection so much? I've never taken rejection well before, but he made me want to keep pursuing him. We began texting each other more and more, a few times a week, and I argued with him constantly about why he was so picky about hanging out. We argued a lot for two people who were not in a relationship and barely had developed a friendship yet, but it was a fun sort of arguing.

I became closer with Catie in hopes of finding out more about what his story was. He was very mysterious to me, and that was extremely intriguing. I was used to guys going after me, but he wasn't like that, and that caused my interest to grow deeper. She told me he couldn't date me because I was still technically married. I tried explaining my situation to her about being separated and how divorce takes a long time, but she was pretty certain he was adamant on keeping that rule. She also told me he was very religious, and even though he had been sexually active in the past, he was now inactive and wanting to wait until marriage. The things she was telling me made it seem like she was trying to talk me out of liking him and back off a bit, and for a while, I started to.

From what she told me, it sounded like it wasn't going to happen for us. I was upset, but I found distractions in other guys I was speaking with. Even though the rejection I felt from him didn't stop me from liking him, it didn't mean I didn't still need to feel that romantic acceptance from other men. I kept myself distracted with others on my bucket list, including the school principal and the much older man who seemed perfect on paper and in looks, but both of which I cried during sex to as I felt pressured into doing it and could not hold back my emotions. At that point, I wasn't doing it to conquer them. I was saying yes to not let them down, and my shame came pouring right out of my eyes. It was so embarrassing, yet they both seemed genuinely interested in me and pursued me afterward, but there were flashbacks from being pressured into sex from my marriage, and I could not shake the feeling and stopped talking to them.

There were two guys with whom I assumed I had sex with but cannot confirm because I was blackout drunk. One was a guitarist of a band I liked, and I woke up naked in bed one morning to others telling me we had sex when I had absolutely no recollection of the sort. The other was in a parking lot outside of a restaurant, where I was left with only slivers of faint pictures in my mind of what was going on, but no recollection of who the person even was, and if there were one or possibly even two of them. I felt wanted in the moments but couldn't shake the feelings of shame, embarrassment, and disgust about myself that followed from allowing myself to be so consumed with alcohol that I had no idea what was being done to my body.

I backed off from hanging out with D for a while as I was occupying my time to date around and surround myself with men who did want me. I didn't talk to him at the gym or on the phone as much anymore. October came, and I invited Catie to my birthday party, and sure enough, D stopped me one day and asked why he wasn't invited. I told him he always was so picky about who he hung out with, and I didn't think he would come to my party, so I didn't want to invite him and get rejected again. He asked to be invited, so I invited him to three different birthday events the last week in

October. He didn't end up coming to any of them of course, but at least, it got us talking again.

We became closer once more, and he and Catie started coming over for dinner every Thursday night. I enjoyed cooking for them, and then we would hang out and watch TV or go in the hot tub or just talk. We became closer each time and started talking more over the phone and through text. He was a good distraction from Reed for me because I was still trying to get over him as well. He started being the person I wanted to talk to before I went to sleep at night and the person I wanted to start talking to the first thing in the morning. Somehow, I felt myself thinking about him when I was out with other guys instead of Reed, and that was a new feeling for me.

I remember the first time he actually asked me to hang out instead of me reaching out first. I was out to lunch with Eric and the kids, and I got a text from him, not even really asking but telling me we were going out that night. I agreed, but Eric decided to have a long talk with me right before I was getting ready to leave, so I ended up being late. It didn't matter as he still managed to get there after me because he was always late. It was just him and I for a while before Catie showed up. I could tell he was uncomfortable because he never could hang out with me alone. One of his rules about how I was still technically married, and even though we were just friends, it wasn't right. He had a lot of rules, which I've come to know as boundaries but knew nothing of the sort at that time. Catie finally showed up, and we went to a bar after we finished eating.

Catie only stayed about forty minutes, so I assumed D was going to be quick to follow her out the door, scared that I would make a move on him or something if we were to be alone. He didn't, however, and we ended up staying out until the bar closed at 2:00 a.m. and had a great time. He wouldn't stop talking about Reed how-ever, like he was jealous of him somehow and wanted me to stop liking him. I was so confused because I thought if you didn't have feelings for someone, why would you go out of your way to say such negative things about the other person she likes? I didn't understand it. I was happy he stayed out with me though and was pleased with just that one small advancement in our friendship. He walked me to my car, gave me a hug goodbye, and we were on our way.

From then on, he wasn't as scared to hang out with me in a one-on-one situation, and we went to dinner, bars, and movies together. It didn't happen often, but if Catie or someone else bailed on us, he usually would still go out with me. He would make it a point to state that we weren't out on a date, but I didn't care. I was still out with him, I enjoyed his company, and for the first time in a long time, it was actually nice spending time with someone who was not trying to get into bed with me. For the first time in a long time, I felt like maybe there was something else about me other than looks that peaked someone's interest, even in an unromantic way. He never made a pass at me, would talk about other girls, and tell me how I shouldn't get divorced, but for some reason, I still felt like we had such a unique connection. I was so sure that connection could have turned into something romantic, but I also was so addicted to love at that point I could have misconstrued the check-out guy at the grocery store saying "Have a great day" with a smile on his face as him trying to flirt.

D introduced me to Christianity, and we started having a lot of conversations about it. I realized I had stepped away from God since my father left, so I started thinking about Him again and added prayer back into my life here and there. I knew I was so lost as I navigated a separation, a pending divorce, figuring out who was going to be leaving our house, how to tell the children, and why I constantly needed the attention of men in my life, or why I constantly needed alcohol in my life. I didn't even know where to begin, and I was too ashamed to even admit to Him the things I've done because I would have to admit them to myself, and I just couldn't do it. I just thought by convincing myself things didn't happen, then God wouldn't know about them either, and I wouldn't have to ask for forgiveness or face them.

D challenged me to remember things I learned from the Catholic church and school growing up, but I hadn't been to church since eighth grade after I had made confirmation, I had to look a lot up on the internet. I even dusted off an old Bible that was sitting in a drawer that had probably never been opened. He quoted scripture, and I argued with him over it, noting the Bible was a book written two thousand years ago, so how in the world could any of it apply to life on Earth as we know it today? A lot of what he was throwing at me dealt with divorce and sexual immorality, two things I was knee-deep in, but we constantly argued over it because of course, I didn't want to hear about how everything I was doing was wrong and how I was committing adultery even though I was "separated." As much as we argued, I will admit he did pique an interest for me in it because it caused me to go into the scripture and try to find verses that would counter his argument about the topic, but he usually ended up being right, although I never told him so.

I began seeing the negative traits about him in a more positive light, once thinking how ridiculous it sounded to be a "born-again virgin," and now being somewhat attracted to that quality. The initial physical attraction I once had for him started to fade away, and I no longer thought about him in a way of lust. I genuinely cared about him and wanted to simply be around him all the time, and there was no longer a feeling of being rejected romantically by him, but a feeling like I was gaining so much more in a different kind of relationship. It was so different than anything I had ever experienced. I wasn't talking to any other guys during this time of a couple of months, nor did I have the desire to meet anyone. I preferred a night in of dinner and meaningful conversation with D in a nonromantic way over a night out drinking at the bar with friends trying to find my next bucket-list conquest. I felt really happy.

One day, in the winter, he texted me, asking if we could talk as I was pulling into a parking spot at Target. Not being able to hear those words without being anxious, I told him he could call me right away. He had a hesitant tone to his voice, like whatever he was about to tell me would affect me somehow and he knew it. He told me he had gotten a new job and was going to be moving to Minnesota. I was devastated. Just as we had reached this point of closeness, he was going to be abandoning me. "Are you going to say something?" he asked. I didn't have any words. Not wanting to sound like a completely pathetic fool, I insincerely told him congratulations. I couldn't stay on the phone with him any longer and told him I needed to go into the store and we could talk later. It felt like God reached down at that moment and ripped my heart out of my body and scolded me for all of my past mistakes. I was just starting to have a relationship with God again, how could He do this to me now?

I went home and started drinking immediately and ended up going out that night with friends. I turned to alcohol to numb the pain I was feeling while I figured out how to deal with what had just been presented to me earlier that day. I started drunk-texting D that night and remembered asking him when he was going to be leaving, a question I wanted to ask earlier but didn't have the words, to which he responded, "Before the Super Bowl." That was next week! How could he leave so soon? I was devastated when I assumed it would be a couple of months. Now I only had a week left with him? How was I supposed to handle all this? I turned to alcohol, depressing music, and writing over the next few days.

I was one of the last people he hung out with that week. He reserved all day on Thursday for me, the day before he left. We went out to breakfast, then I sat with him while he got a pedicure, then we went to a movie and said our goodbyes. A little while later though, he asked if I wanted to meet him and Catie and some others out at the bar for one last night, so I begged my babysitter to stay, and I went back out that night. I needed to spend every last moment I could with him before I would probably never see or talk to him again. I grieved my loss for several days, but it wasn't long before I started going back out, drinking, and searching for the next man to make me feel better and fill this new void I had in my life now that D was not around.

CHAPTER 8

The Move

November 16, 2018

Jamaica. I know I say this a lot, but this trip was life-changing. Or was it simply getting a massage a couple of weeks ago and Dave suggesting this book I listen to, and I just happened to be at the exact part of the book at the exact point coming home from this trip that led me to this decision? It's really crazy how things come together. I am not sure I'll ever understand it. Anna, Christine, and I had the most amazing week. I can't even talk about the guys I met down there right now. That will have to be a separate entry on a separate day. I have too much else on my mind right now. Flying home today, I had the realization that I need to be the one to leave our house. Eric is holding on to it as a way to hold on to me because I told him I would never leave if we couldn't agree on who got to keep the house. That I would suck it up and stay in the marriage for the sake of the kids and staying in the neighborhood. I fully intended on following through with that plan in the hopes he would get frustrated after so long and be the one to leave. Until tonight. I reached a part in the book that talked about being on your deathbed and looking back on your life and wondering if you stayed in an unhealthy marriage or a job that made you miserable just for the security. I am not sure if I remember any other parts of that book, but that sentence changed my life today.

I told Anna and Christine in the car ride back home of my decision. I was confident in telling them, and for the first time, I did not feel anxious or uneasy about the unknown road ahead. I now look at it with a certain strength that this is what I have to do, and everything is going to be all right. I was a horrible person this week, with all the drinking and guys, but somehow, I felt taken care of tonight. I have no idea where I will move to or what I will be able to afford or how I will break the news to Eric or the children, but I know things are going to work out now. I think I can rest easy now, but not before I say a little prayer to God. Good night.

*****

After a couple of years of separation with Eric, I took a girl's trip to Jamaica with Anna and Christine, my friends from the gym. It was an unbelievable week filled with laughter, sunshine, and fun. I had a big part in picking the destination honestly because I was thinking about Jamaican guys and reggae music. Anna and Christine were both in relationships, but of course, I was not, so I was excited to see if I could conquer any bucket-list guys on this trip as well. I didn't have as much freedom at home, still living with Eric, so this was my chance to let loose without having to tiptoe around. With a one-track mind and an all-inclusive drink package, I had my share of "fun" and allowed myself once again to fall victim to the flesh of a beautiful Jamaican man.

After reflecting on the week and listening to a book on the plane ride home, I came to the realization that I would have to move out of my house, something I never thought I would have to do. My sights were now focused on this new venture, and I told Eric the day after I got back. Part of him thought he at least had the house to hold over my head as a way of getting me to stay, so I know sadness and loss of control came over him but, at the same time, comfort in knowing he would be able to stay at the home, and I was okay with that.

The next couple of weeks were disappointment after disappointment after seeing what I would actually be able to afford. I wanted desperately to stay in our neighborhood because that is what made it our home. All my efforts over the years in organizing play-dates, firepits, cookouts, neighborhood outings, and making sure the kids always had someone to play with and I always had another mom to confide in, would be for nothing if I moved out of the neighborhood and didn't see everyone as much. Houses that I could afford were either along busy streets or in a townhouse development with no yard for my kids to play in. Resentment started growing toward Eric because I knew I would have the kids a majority of the time, and I couldn't believe he would allow himself to keep that big house for the little time he would even have them or be home.

One night, I was hosting a playdate at our house, and I made the announcement to everyone that I would be moving. It was very hard for me, but everyone was really supportive. One of the husbands happened to be there that night, and he informed me that the neighbors across from their house were thinking about putting their house up for sale sometime in the future. This seemed too good to be true. He rarely ever even came to our playdates, and he happened to be there this time to inform me of this. I found the owners information on Facebook and sent him a message inquiring about it. I anxiously waited several days and had almost given up when the owner texted me back. Within a few days, I had gone over and looked at the house; and within a few weeks, not thinking I could ever afford something in our neighborhood, they had accepted my offer, which was a lot under market since we didn't have to use a realtor. I would be moving six houses away from Eric in the same neighborhood!

Telling the kids was one of the most difficult things I have had to do in my entire life. They didn't know about us getting a divorce or me moving out prior. I had slept in the guest room for years, but they still only thought of us as married. I will never forget Kayla's reaction. She immediately screamed and cried out and ran downstairs. Greg's reaction was just as memorable. He left the room quietly and came back with a bag packed with a couple pairs of pants and shirts, ready to "move" to mommy's house. It lightened the mood a bit to see the perspective of a nonverbal, special needs six-year-old. I would say the only saving grace for me that day was being able to tell them I would only be moving six houses up the street, and we could go visit the new house that day for them to pick out their bedrooms. We were all being taken care of that difficult day somehow in some way.

Even though we had been separated for a couple of years, and I still went out and did my own thing, it wasn't until after I moved out and we were in the process of divorce that I felt fully ready to "date." It started turning from shameful sexual conquests and secretive meet-ups to being completely free to go out on real dates in search of some real potential. My intentions were more genuine at that point, but it didn't mean my actions fully aligned with them that summer. I still needed the attention from multiple guys to ease the loneliness when my children stayed at Eric's house and I was by myself. Each night I didn't have my children, I made sure to have plans either with a guy or with friends to potentially meet a guy. I was back to a one-track mind and was fully focused on finding love. I even went as far as creating an online dating profile for the fun of it one night while out with my friend. Because there were no cute guys out at the bar we were at, we went online and entertained ourselves by "swiping."

I never had a shortage of guys wanting to hang out. Even if I wasn't into them physically, I still went out with them, so I wasn't alone. On the rare nights I was home early or didn't have anything to do, three guys at a time would be texting me, so at least I still had validation and felt like I was in a relationship. Even though Eric and I were separated, I was still living at our house for those years, so being on my own was a whole new state of being for me. I felt free, yet alone.

The Ex-Boyfriend's Roommate

When I was in my first relationship with Matt at seventeen, we had such a special connection and love for one another, but problems arose anytime we would hang out with his friends. I was mature for my age, and he was immature for his age, so it seemed like the perfect fit for us but his friends didn't think so, and we would fight a lot about it.

After two years, I finally couldn't take it anymore. We hung out with his friends a lot, but some of them seemed to have strong feelings of dislike toward me, and I could never figure out why. It got to a point where they would be so mean to me I would start crying, and it created separation between Matt and I because he obviously did not want to have to choose between his friends and I, nor did I ever make him. It just became so unbearable to try and hang out with them, it would end up causing fights between him and I because he would choose his friends almost every time. I broke up with him and started dating Eric immediately after.

Fast-forward sixteen years, I had kept in touch with one of Matt's old friend, Brayden. He was always sweet to me, so a few years back, we reconnected over some drinks and stayed in touch since. One night, we were out at a bar and I was asking about the rest of Matt's old friends and asked if he kept in touch with any of them still. "I just went out with Brent last night actually." I asked how he was doing, and he told me him and another guy Darren were out in town and asking him to meet them out right then and there.

"Tell them you'll meet them out there, but don't tell them I am coming," I said as I was curious to meet up with them. Brent was Matt's roommate for the two years I was dating him, so I saw a lot of him, but he wasn't always coming out with us and didn't really seem to have a problem with me. Darren, however, was horrible to me before he walked through the door the first time he even met me. It had bothered me for seventeen years what I did to cause him to treat me the way he did because I could not recall one thing. I am sure I had my moments of immaturity and jealousy that arose from the age gap and knowing he was out at the bars a lot while I was studying calculus in high school, but I had always been a nice person and did love Matt. All these years had passed, however, and I was curious to see how he would react to me now. I was in a different place in my life at this point, a much happier and grown-up place, so I no longer really cared about what peers from my teenage years thought about me.

"Surprise!" as we walked into the bar. I couldn't forget the look of shock on their faces, but I didn't even give them a chance to react. I went right in to hug Brent and gave Darren a colder but friendly nod. "Hello, Darren."

As we moved to a table, Brent and I started catching up immediately. He was one of the few friends who had never treated me badly, so I was genuinely interested in what he had been up to the past sixteen years. We bonded immediately over our love of dogs, music, and our respective divorces. It was quite unexpected and a little unusual, but there was definitely a little chemistry there between us as he gazed at me with his piercing blue eyes.

Before we knew it, midnight was approaching, and Brent said he was heading back down to Florida, where he was living now, the next morning. We all decided to pack it in, yet I was feeling a little incomplete as I was not ready for the night to end. Brayden drove me back home, but on the way, I did something I almost never did. I friend requested Brent on social media. Within seconds, he messaged me, and apparently, he was doing the same. I knew we had a connection and so began our back-and-forth flirty texts both alluding to the fact that we weren't ready for the night to end. After about twenty minutes, I finally made the move and said, "Why don't you come over so we can continue the conversation in person?"

"On my way," he texted back almost immediately. I quickly scrambled to straighten up my bedroom and freshen up my body because something came over me that night with him, and I knew what lay ahead for me.

He was at my door within ten minutes. He walked in, and I nervously made small talk with him for a minute before he pulled my body into his and passionately kissed me. After tingles were sent down my body, he pulled away and said, "I need a drink," and I laughed and poured us each a glass of wine.

I took him for a tour around my house, then we ended up in my family room and sat on a couch conversing while listening to music in the background. He was easy to talk to, and we had a surprising amount of things in common. I felt really comfortable around him but also really turned on at the same time. We both kept going back to the fact that we knew each other so long ago and, never in a million years, thought this would be happening right now. He did admit to hoping I was coming out that night with Brayden since he had heard I started hanging out with him again, so I was a little surprised and flattered.

While the conversation was nice, the tingles came over me again, and I couldn't ignore the feelings inside of my body. I don't know if it was the "bad-boy" persona or the taboo of making out with my ex-boyfriend's roommate, but I wanted him right then. I noticed the window was open behind him, so I put my left leg over his waist, and I said, "Oh sorry, I was getting a little chilly, so I need to close the window." He groaned for a second then grabbed me with both hands and squeezed tight to pull me back down to kiss him again.

We started shedding each other's clothes, when out of nowhere, he felt the need to tell me it had been about a year since he had been with anyone, which was his ex-wife he had gotten divorced from around that time. Suddenly, the bad-boy roommate had a softer, more sensitive side to him, and what may have turned other girls off made me even more into him.

It was actually a really nice night. For someone who didn't really ever enjoy sex, something about him made me want to keep going and not say over and over in my head, *Can this be over yet?* We would pass out for a few minutes in between, but then I wanted to kiss him again, and it would start all over. I saw such a different side of him than what I was used to. He was apologizing about how out of prac-tice he was, but I kept reassuring him that he was amazing. I don't know if it was a ploy to get me to boost his confidence, but what would normally be annoying I thought was kind of cute because he was so nervous around me.

Besides a raging hangover from wine and no sleep, the next morning brought some interesting feelings. Normally, I would have felt somewhat ashamed for sleeping with someone so quick; but for some reason, I felt kind of content with it. Even though we hadn't spoken in sixteen years, I still felt like I've known him for so long, and he was someone I had spent almost every day with for two years while I was dating Matt. He was also going back to Florida that day, so I felt like that was our only chance. It wasn't like we were going to start dating since he lived around here, in which case, I probably would have waited… Well, who am I kidding? I was drunk, and that's what I did, so probably not.

He ended up texting me a few hours later while waiting for his plane to arrive, apologizing for the awkward exit. It made me smile to hear from him, at least it appeared I didn't get used at all. Over the next several days, we learned more about each other back and forth through texts. He told me he needed a drink that night because he was so nervous to be with me. It had been a long time for him, and he couldn't believe I would be into him in that way.

Even though it started out as a one-night stand, I think our feelings grew for each other after the fact, and it became nice to connect with someone who has been through the divorce process. I felt like I helped him through his depression and anxiety and taught him life tricks to get him back on track. We continued to text, and he continued to make me smile every time I talked to him, but the distance was hard. Of course, those who I developed feelings for always leave. If others come up around here, ultimately if it's easier to see someone, the closer you can grow with that person and the further you become from the long-distance person. It was a nice change of pace to be with someone I did actually like and who seemed to genuinely like me though, so I had a glimmer of hope.

The Reality TV Personality

That summer, I signed up to go to an adult summer camp for the second year in a row. I had gone the year before with Anna, and we had the time of our lives. It was everything I dreamed an overnight summer camp would have been like as a kid but throw in drinking and single guys, and it was better than I could have imagined at that stage in my life. She was supposed to go back with me this time, but she ended up back in a relationship, and this was definitely more of a single's camp. I convinced my other friend and her boyfriend to go, but they ended up backing out just a week prior to the camp. I decided to go by myself anyway, which is something I was absolutely terrified of, but I had already paid and could use the weekend away.

They sent an email out beforehand, letting us know a studio was going to be taping a reality television show there that summer, and we would need to fill out waivers if we wanted to opt in or out of being on camera. I didn't think I was interesting enough to actually end up on camera since I was so shy and there by myself, so I was fine with it. The first night after arrival, I went down and found some people I knew from last year and immediately felt more comfortable. I started drinking and loosening up, and the cameras started coming out, and the stars of the reality show were coming down the hill. I didn't even pay attention and continued my conversations. Garrett caught my eye because he was tall and dark and stood out among the rest of the Caucasian New England crowd. I must have caught his as well as he came over and started talking with me and complementing me on my smile.

We hung out a lot that night, but I didn't realize until hours later that he was one of the stars on the show. I think he must have told me, but I was too intoxicated to comprehend. We kissed that first night in private, but as we walked out of the room, there was an entire camera crew on us; and at that point, I realized I was the object of affection for one of the stars that weekend, and that made me really nervous. He was pretty intoxicated himself, which was a turnoff for me, so I ended up leaving the area he was and going to hang out with different people I had met.

The next day, I found a new group to hang out with, and we went about our day and participated in things like slip 'n' slide kickball and softball. Garrett and the camera crew were at volleyball when we made our way there. They filmed us getting to know each other in a sober way as we played. I was skeptical of how genuine his intentions were since cameras were constantly on him, but I played along and actually had a barrier up for the first time in a while, until I started drinking again of course. I was pretty wild that night. I danced on tables, drank a lot, and kept sneaking off with Garrett to make out away from the cameras. They kept finding us though, so the night became a game of hide-and-seek because I did not want to be on television kissing someone or doing anything that I was doing that night for that matter.

After the dance ended, we made plans for him to come back to my cabin. He snuck out of his cabin and came down, but there were cameras waiting for him. He told them they could film him coming into my cabin but wanted the microphones off him when he came in so they agreed. The next few hours were wonderful. We talked about everything, and he was a perfect gentleman. I don't even think we kissed while he was inside. My roommate came back, and then the three of us talked together until the early morning hours. I actually developed feelings for him that night and was shocked he had so many questions about me, like he actually cared.

Everyone was leaving Sunday afternoon, and the camera men were all over us, trying to get some juicy farewell on camera. I refused. I am sure they were disappointed with Garrett's "pick" for the week as I am sure any other girl would have jumped at the chance to be on television and flashed herself before it, but I am extremely camera shy and certainly didn't need my kids, friends, or clients at home knowing what I do for fun on the weekends. So I gave him a quick hug, and we were both on our way.

Within the hour of us leaving, he started texting me; and over the next few days, we talked and texted and really got to know each other. We made plans for me to go visit him in New York City. We began seeing each other without all the cameras, and I really started developing feelings for him. I learned he really was a genuine guy and was not just into me for sex or the cameras since we had not slept together that weekend. We developed a friendship, but when we saw each other, the benefits were there, but it was always me who went to visit him. He never came to visit me and that bothered me, so I started getting frustrated and began pushing him away a little bit at a time. I did have others I was speaking with, and he was another state away, so allowing the communication to still go on did the trick for me at that time, even though I knew it wasn't going to be going anywhere.

There were more. I wish I could say this was as many as I was with, but there were a few others. The masseur, the guy who was ten years younger than me, the popular guy from high school who never spoke to me, you name it. I touched on pretty much all the clichés and was involved romantically with all of them in some way, shape, or form. Many times I felt used; many times I felt like I was using them. Most guys did seem to have a genuine interest in me, but after sleeping with them, I no longer had an interest in them, and I had no idea why. I liked to come off to others as some conqueror of men in some woman-empowering way to get back at all the ones who rejected or abandoned me in the past, but deep down, I didn't exactly feel good about playing with other people's emotions. Even if they genuinely cared about me and sought a relationship with me and even though I fully consented to giving them my body, with the aid of alcohol of course, it was almost as though I punished them for allowing it to happen on the first date or shortly after. I almost wanted to go through all these men and subconsciously give them each a test to see if they were willing to stop it before it started. Those who did always got away. I was drawn to that sexual rejection but, at the same time, was offended by it, which made me test and push harder to see if they would cave in and, in turn, made them turn away from me. There were very few of those, maybe one or two, but I had no idea at the time why I was so drawn to them.

CHAPTER 9

The One?

September 23, 2019

By now I am realizing I have a problem. I am going after these total clichés. Well, I shouldn't say I am necessarily seeking them out, but I keep finding myself in these situations, and I don't think I can even tell my friends anymore because I am feeling more and more shame.

One night of the festival, I was pretty out of it. One too many poolside mimosas, and I was trying everything in my power to keep the room from spinning, so I wasn't really thinking about guys that night or anything else for that matter.

By the second night, I was ready to let loose, partake in some more beverages, and have a great time. I noticed John's mesmerizing gaze while Erin and I were in line. He was serving everyone in front of me but couldn't take his eyes off me. I remembered him from the night before because he was bartending next to the lady who's line we kept going in yesterday. Come to think of it, I was starting to recall the glares from him yesterday. "Hi, beautiful, what can I get for you?" I shyly looked down for a second before I gave him my order. Soon enough, John and I had exchanged numbers, and he was coming back to our house after he finished up work that night. I can't make it through a fun event or a weekend away without being with a guy. I need it to feel fulfilled, like I've won something, but why do I still feel empty now? These are fun stories to tell, and my friends all love hearing about them, but I am left feeling alone, even when the guys continue to pursue me after the fact. I was no longer interested in them in that way after that first night, but it's nice to have guys texting me throughout the day. I have this companionship without having to deal with being a slave to someone at home. It had felt like freedom in the past, but now my freedom was starting to feel more like emptiness.

*****

I had been hanging out with Erin a lot recently. I was single and always up for having fun or simply being a drinking buddy for her. She was going through things in her life and marriage and really enjoyed the companionship of a girl always up for doing things. We were hanging out in early September, and we were talking about the guys I was dating. This was always a hot topic among my married friends living vicarious through me, but they were also content with the steadiness of their marriages at the same token. She mentioned to me that she told her friend Matthew that he should ask me out on a date, but he had just broken up with his girlfriend, so he wasn't really ready to date yet. I knew to whom she was referring but couldn't place his exact face. I knew I had met him before and thought he was adorable but couldn't remember exactly what he looked like. I had seen him at a couple of their parties and remember being drawn to him, but he had had a girlfriend, so it didn't go beyond my glares at his handsomeness, which were quite frequent. The conversation ended there, but I kept it in the back of my mind.

The next weekend, Erin and I had gone to a music festival at the Jersey Shore for a long weekend. We had an incredible time: listening to music on the beach, laying down and looking up at the stars, and hanging out with all her friends from college, who were there from Pittsburg. Erin and I were really close, but this was the first time we had actually gone away together and really had a chance to bond. I never felt closer to her. I would say it was one of my favorite weekends of my life, and one that would be the last before my life would change forever.

I ended up meeting someone at the festival of course. Anywhere I went that summer, I ended up meeting someone. I wasn't looking for it this time. I was really enjoying girl time, but I couldn't escape his gaze. He was one of the guys serving drinks and couldn't keep his eyes off me. They were dark and piercing; he was tall and seemed older, a bigger guy. Not my usual type. After he got off work, he found me. We hang out that night. Why couldn't I get through one night or weekend out without needing some guy to make me feel better? I was embarrassed to what I did and played it off like nothing happened when Erin asked. I had again felt ashamed for what I did.

Two days after we got back from the trip, I got a call from Erin, telling me that her brother-in-law had passed away suddenly. It was devastating. He had two young boys. I didn't know what to say, but I knew I wanted to be there for both of them as much as I could. I was over their house almost every day that week, different people coming and going each day and night. I was close with Erin's husband Kyle as well, whose brother it was. I felt the need to be over there as much as possible to comfort them. The funeral was a week later, and I rode with one of our other friends from the neighborhood to attend. We were just going to pay our respects to the family then head out, but for some reason, we ended up staying for the service. I couldn't help but look around for this Matthew guy Erin was telling me about. What was wrong with me? I was at a funeral service, and I was looking around to see if there was a cute guy in the pews!

It was a beautiful service, and we hung around for a little afterward, making sure we said our goodbyes. Erin invited us to the burial and the luncheon afterward. I wanted to go, but Lisa had driven me, and we had already decided to go out to lunch in town after anyway. I told her we had already made plans and maybe I would see them later. I had forgotten something back inside the church, so I went back in for a minute, and in going back in, I ended up crossing paths and locking eyes with a tall handsome man; it was Matthew.

The funeral had Lisa and I thinking a lot about our deaths and how our funerals would go. It made for very interesting conversation at lunch. We were wrapping things up, and I had the sudden urge to want to go to the family luncheon Erin had invited us to. It was on a Wednesday, so it was the only day I didn't have my kids, and I had already taken off work, so I had nothing to do the rest of the day anyway. I wanted to be there to support one of my best friends. After Lisa dropped me off, I got right into my car and drove to the banquet hall, where they were holding the luncheon. I was very late, so I felt extremely uncomfortable walking in, but luckily, there was a spot for me with Lisa's side of the family. Or unluckily…they were heavy drinkers of course, and I had never really been to a funeral before, so what did I do? I kept going to the bar and buying these people carafes of wine! What else was I good for anyway? I knew how to drink, have a good time, and make people laugh. These were all defense mechanisms because I didn't think I was good enough to offer anything else.

It was on about the second time up to the bar when I saw one of Erin's husband's friends Tom standing up there talking to this Matthew guy, so I said hello and gave him a hug. Then I turned to Matthew, trying to gauge whether he remembered me or not. It seemed like maybe he did, so I said hello and how it was nice to see him again. He was more handsome than I remembered. He had gray pants on with a white button-down collared shirt that was unbuttoned at the top. No tie. Sunglasses around the back of his head, around his collar. We went back to our respective tables as he sat a couple of tables away from me with the rest of Kyle's friends from high school and soccer.

His gaze was piercing. I tried to keep focus on the conversations at my table, but I could feel his eyes on me. Every time I looked up and back at him, he didn't turn away, but rather kept his gaze and had just the slightest glimpse of a smile expression on his face. As outgoing as I seem around a group of guys, especially when I am drinking, I am actually pretty shy at heart. I hadn't been drunk at that point anyway, so I didn't really know how to handle the gaze. I would look at him, and when he kept staring, I would give a little smile back, but only as I looked back down onto my plate. This back and forth went on for a while. If I looked over at him and he wasn't looking right then, only moments later would he look back at me again. Everyone seemed to be having conversations around us at our tables, the room was loud and noisy, yet we seemed to be the only two people there. Gosh, he was handsome. Clean-shaven, tall, thin, brown hair and eyes. Those eyes. I felt like I could see right into those eyes even from across the room. Yes. This was the guy I remember meeting at the party and he had a girlfriend, and I remembered being disappointed.

After the luncheon wrapped up, many of the closer family and friends stuck around and went to the downstairs bar at the facility. By this time, I had a few glasses of wine in me and was ready for more. There was no shortage of Kyle's friends there willing to buy me another glass. I was wearing a black dress, probably showing a little more cleavage than funeral appropriate, but it was the most proper black dress I owned. The next one would have been a short cock-tail dress with spaghetti straps. The guys certainly didn't complain. Matthew sat at a high-top table, and I sat next to him. We started talking immediately, and I felt an instant connection to him. Who really knows though, four or five glasses of wine in. All I probably knew at that point was that he was so handsome, and I wanted him.

I continued to do the only thing I knew how to do in getting a guy's attention, and that was to act drunk and ditsy, laugh and smile a lot, and flirt with every guy around. I let them tease me. I may have laughed and said "Stop that!" in a flirty manner. That's all I knew. I didn't have anything else to offer. I only wanted Matthew's attention though. I kept him in my sight, out of the corner of my eye every time I was talking to someone else. Since I didn't have anything else to offer as far as intellectual conversation at that point, I figured I would let him observe me being flirty with the other guys so he would see how much I was wanted and want me for himself. I don't remember much else for the rest of the time at the bar except not wanting the night to end. Apparently, I made out with him outside, but I do not even remember this. Our first kiss, and I didn't remember. How much wine did I have?

I was somehow able to convince Kyle to have people back to their house afterward, but there was no way I was going to be able to drive. Tom had seen the obvious connection Matthew and I had made at that point and offered to have Matthew drive me back while he drove my car. I started sobering up at this point and remembered parts of the way back to my house. Matthew was sweet. He wasn't drunk at all. He told me about what he did for a living, even though I didn't really understand. I wanted to change out of my dress and into sweats since we were just going back to Erin and Kyle's, and that's what I usually wore there. I must have immediately felt comfortable with Matthew to be able to quickly want to put sweats on. He came into my kitchen and kissed me immediately up against the island. I had to stop him so I could get changed and head over to their house. We came upstairs and started kissing wildly in the middle of my bedroom floor. As we were kissing, he started walking us toward the bed and leaned over me. I had enough sense at that point to stop him. I don't know if it was because I wanted to get over to Erin's house or if I was nervous about having sex with him already or if it was too much too fast, but I stopped it from getting any further than kissing at that point, and we got changed and headed over.

What would have happened if I slept with him right then and there? What if we didn't go to Erin's house and spent the night getting to know each other? The first of many what-ifs I would spend the next two years going over and over in my head. Matthew probably wouldn't have gotten drunk that night if we stayed at my house. As I was sobering up, he just kept drinking whiskey and smoking cigarettes over at their house. I hated cigarettes. Why did I still like him even if he smoked? Even though we had just basically met that afternoon, it felt almost like we were in a relationship with each other already. Everyone else was coupled up anyway, so it almost seemed fitting, and I liked the idea. It was just for that night though. I couldn't help but think to myself how far this would really go with as much drinking as each of us did, him getting drunk and smoking all those cigarettes. Plus, he couldn't help but talk about how much his ex-girlfriend ripped his heart out. I still liked him, but I grew tired quickly that night, especially after I started having to be the last remaining adult since everyone was falling further into drunkenness, even though I was younger than everyone by six or seven years. I told him he could stay at my house since it was about 1:00 a.m., and he was not able to drive home at that point.

Any hesitations I had before escaped me at this point as it was 1:00 a.m., and I was faced with yet another man who had his sights after me, and mine absolutely on him. *This is just what people do nowadays*, I told myself again. He was expecting it and would be disappointed if I didn't give him what he wanted. I was tired, he was drunk, but I really wanted him to like me, so I slept with him.

An alarm that wasn't mine went off around five thirty that morning, and if I wasn't fully awake from that, it was the loud cursing that came immediately afterward from this man next to me, who leapt up and put on his clothes faster than I could even open my eyes. I think he may have said goodbye, but it was all a hurried blur; but either way, he was out the door fast as I guessed he was going to be late for work.

It had occurred to me that we never exchanged numbers the previous night when Erin texted me that afternoon, saying Matthew had asked her for my number. I guess that was somewhat good news. I wasn't used as a one-night stand, and maybe he really does have interest in me. He texted the next day, and we made plans to hang out on Saturday night after I participated in the Philadelphia Dragon Boat Festival all day.

I had been drinking pretty much all day since 8:00 a.m. as that is when the event started. Our team won our division, and we were on such a high that even after the event, we went back to one of the guys' houses and continued the celebration at night by his firepit. A few of us were dropped off, and Matthew had offered to come pick us up as he was at some sort of sober event at his church. So here we were on our second "meeting," and I started out drunk, and he was sober. I had always been shy, especially around guys so the alcohol caused me to let loose, become more outgoing and flirtier—something I assumed guys wanted. After all, I was enamored with him and didn't think I was good enough, so I needed all the outside help I could get. That night, we hung out at my house with Erin and Kyle since they were all friends. It seemed perfect. I started seeing flashes of the future with fun times and double dates with our mutual best friends. Matthew started drinking at my house, and before we knew it, we were both back to where we had been on the first night, practically a repeat.

He texted me the next day and asked for a do-over. "Okay, two strikes against me. You have to give me another chance to prove myself," he said. As if I cared about whether he finished or how he performed, I was only sleeping with him because I wanted to give him what he wanted. I never really enjoyed sex before anyway; it was all the same to me. But I did think it was cute that he felt like he had something to make up to me.

At this point, I was still communicating with the reality star, music-festival bartender, and ex-boyfriend's old roommate. I was actually supposed to go visit reality guy in New York City the next night. He actually called me as I was pulling up to Matthew's street and needed to reschedule for another day that week. For some reason, I did not care. He was the one I had liked the most, but I was so excited to be seeing Matthew that it didn't matter. I didn't end up rescheduling that night. I just said we could talk another day and quickly rushed him off the phone as I was excited to start my night. It was like I was being told to forget him and enter this date with a blank slate. None of the guys were serious, and none of them lived anywhere close, so they were more of a "texting" relationship. Nevertheless, they kept me occupied as Matthew certainly wasn't "over-pursuing" me by calling or texting all day long, which I liked. And we had two drunk hangouts, the first of which was meeting at a funeral. Let's be honest, where was this going?

I pulled up to the address he gave me, which was right along the main street in town. I showed up on time, but he wasn't prepared for that I guess as he said he hadn't showered or anything yet. I didn't care. I was just so excited to be there. He took me up to his apartment and showed me around the small one-bedroom place he had just moved into but a few weeks prior. It was nice and cozy and just seeing the smile in his eyes as he was so proud of his place, and I loved that about him immediately. He seemed a little nervous as he was cooking something up for us, like he was trying to impress me. I've had guys cook for me before, but it seemed more to show off than to just do something nice for me. I sat on the couch in the living room as I turned around to watch and talk with him while he cooked. He was wearing a plain green long-sleeved T-shirt and gray athletic shorts and bare feet. He looked perfect to me.

Although I had brought a bottle of wine, I sipped slowly. For the first time, we were having a real date and real conversation. I didn't feel like I needed the "extra help." He asked if I was seeing anyone else, and I was honest about the guys I was talking with. He told me about his breakup, and I told him about the divorce I was going through. He told me how he had a drunk-driving incident that nearly killed him ten years prior and how his brother was a recovering drug and alcohol addict, who was also in prison. Neither one of us held much back that first real date night, and I don't think either of us were turned off. We ended up walking to a local bar and continued our conversation with some more drinks. We didn't go overboard this time, but things definitely loosened up. I started feeling something I never really felt before. I could not stop gazing into his eyes and picturing a future together. Could I already be falling in love with this guy?

I slept over that night, and if I was going based off his goals for that night, I would say he more than made up for his first two strikes. This time felt different. I actually enjoyed it, and I didn't feel upset with myself afterward, like just about every guy I had ever been with prior. Not that I did the first two times with him, but I was more just going through the motions and didn't really think about it too much. He had to be at work by 6:00 a.m. every day, so I had to get up and get out by five thirty, but I was on such an emotional high I didn't really care, and I certainly couldn't go back to sleep when I got back to my house. He was all I could think about for the next couple of days. They were kind of an emotional blur of feelings, like falling in love, but I don't think we really even talked much. I had people over one night, and I told everyone this was the love of my life. Eight days of knowing each other, three nights of hanging out, and one real date. Everyone thought I was crazy, but I didn't care. I just knew it. I tried not being a typical needy girl and didn't text him too much. Erin had texted me the following Saturday, saying she was inviting people over and had invited Matthew, so I was ecstatic. I had family in town visiting, but I went over to her house in hopes to see Matthew again. A few hours went by, and he was still not there. No one had heard from him, so I tried texting him as well but received no response. Although I had fun with my friends, I was disappointed that he had not come. He got back to me about 1:00 a.m. that morning, saying he hadn't been feeling well. Something didn't feel right.

CHAPTER 10

Back to Worldly Distractions

November 30, 2019

Dear Matthew,

I came across a song the other day that really resonated with me. I want you to listen to it whenever you are feeling unsure about my feelings for you. Over and over, if you have to. I am going to write out the lyrics for you so you have them as well. When you listen to it, think back on that night in New Jersey after the party when we were sitting in your car, talking. If I could describe what was going through my head in that moment, this song would be it. It explains everything and all my feelings. Enjoy!

"I Was Made for Loving You," by Tori Kelly

A dangerous plan, just this time
A stranger's hand clutched in mine
I'll take this chance, so call me blind
I've been waiting all my life

Please don't scar this young heart
Just take my hand
I was made for loving you
Even though we may be hopeless hearts just pass-
    ing through
Every bone screaming, I don't know what we
    should do
All I know is, darling, I was made for loving you
Hold me close, through the night
Don't let me go, we'll be all right
Touch my soul and hold it tight
I've been waiting all my life
I won't scar your young heart
Just take my hand
'Cause I was made for loving you
Even though we may be hopeless hearts just pass-
    ing through
Every bone screaming I don't know what we
    should do
All I know is, darling, I was made for loving you
Please don't go, I've been waiting so long
Oh, you don't even know me at all
But I was made for loving you
I was made for loving you
Even though we may be hopeless hearts just pass-
    ing through
Every bone screaming, I don't know what we
    should do
All I know is, darling, I was made for loving you.

*****

Three days went by without hearing from him. What was wrong? I know I wasn't being overbearing because I didn't text him either. Was I in the middle of us each "playing the game"? I didn't want to be. I never liked that. I knew what my feelings were and wanted to go forward with them, but from prior experience, I also know I can't be too much too soon. I finally texted him on that Wednesday and said a simple "Good morning" around 8:00 or 9:00 a.m. When 5:00 p.m. hit and he still hadn't texted back, I finally said something to him along the lines of "Okay then. I hope you had a great day and have a great night." I used my typical sarcasm, but I realized I had been the victim of this "ghosting" everyone was talking about, and I was not happy about it. What had I done? Was it because I slept with him on our first night? He's the one who initiated it. Was I somehow supposed to know I should have had better morals and rejected him? Then he may have been frustrated with me, and I didn't want to be responsible for frustrating anyone. Did he only stick around for that third meetup to prove that he was able to perform sexually after the first two failed attempts and was planning on not sticking around the whole time? Was our conversation all fake at his house? Did he get turned off by my honesty about dating other guys? I swear I texted all of them in the two or three days after our date that I was seeing someone. I didn't want any of them. I wanted Matthew. I just got finished telling everyone he was the love of my life. Now I was left feeling like a broken and used fool. I needed to get out of the house and cope with all these feelings of sudden shock and insecurity. I called my friend Jackie.

We went out that night, and I hit the bar hard. "Why wasn't I good enough?" I kept asking. Jackie hadn't even met the guy yet and she already didn't like him because he was hurting me by ghosting me. He was forty-four years old. I wasn't even aware men his age even did that. I thought that was something the twenty-year-olds did. I was so confused, but the wine was numbing my pain and insecurities. Next, I turned to my phone contacts.

It had been a while since I reached out to Reed. I was so busy with the other guys I was dating that I hadn't spoken to him since the last time we were together. We started flirty texting back and forth until it was established. I would go to his house. Jackie tried to stop me since I had a ton to drink, but I knew the alcohol would wear off, and I would be back to hurting again. I needed a man to make me feel better about the man I actually liked, whom obviously didn't like me back.

Somehow I made it to his apartment. He was in a different one. It had been so long I didn't even know he moved. It was like old times again. We caught up, watched a movie, and then slept together. I didn't sleep at all that night with him next to me. Why didn't I feel any better? Why was I still thinking about Matthew? I couldn't get him out of my head. Why had he still not responded to me? I couldn't wait to get out of there. As soon as it was light enough, I started getting ready to leave. I said goodbye and left, and not one minute later, Reed called me and asked if he could make me breakfast. *Make me breakfast?* He never offered to do that before. The one time I was actually eager to get home. *To get home to what though? Sit and wait for Matthew not to call me?* I went back in and anxiously waited for breakfast to be ready so I could eat and then leave. It was really sweet of him, but where was that ever before?

I needed to speak with Erin. Maybe she heard from Matthew and could give me any insight to this situation. I just wanted to be back home so I could gain some clarity. Reed always made me feel better. I always felt like he was using me, but this time, I think I used him. I used him to try and get over another guy and make myself feel better, but that did not work this time. I just wanted Matthew. Tired, hungover, and depressed, I laid in bed the rest of the day, waiting to hear back from Erin, Matthew, or anyone. At 2:30 p.m., I received a text from Matthew, asking if he could come over to talk. *Oh, boy.*

I greeted him at my door, and he knew what he had done to me. "How are you doing?" he asked.

"I'm okay," I said, lying. Clearly I was miserable, heartbroken, and anxious.

"So we are really attracted to each other, right?" he asked.

"Yeah," I answered, trying to gauge his nervous body language to figure out what he was getting at. I could tell immediately it wasn't anything good. I invited him inside to my family room and nervously sat on the couch opposite from him. The next thirty-five minutes were somewhat of a blur as I was trying to stay composed and not lose it in front of this man I barely knew but, at the same time, thought I was in love with. He explained that he had come to Christ right before he met me and started on a path to walk with him but through all these circumstances starting with his friend's death, he had met me and inadvertently caused him to go back to his old ways, which were against this new life he was trying to live. He hadn't been healed from his past relationship yet, and he did not want to hurt me since we jumped into things so quickly.

Everything he was saying made sense to me, but it didn't mean I liked it. After his spiel, I asked him if we could still be friends. I knew right then, more than ever, he was worth waiting for, and I was willing to take a huge step back and get to know each other as friends. I remembered things D taught me about Christianity and remembered telling myself I wanted to be with a Christian man. I didn't even know what that meant or entailed at the time, but I just knew I loved that in D, and now here was a man I could have had but was ending things because I wasn't Christian enough for him. Why wasn't I good enough for any of these guys I actually saw value in?

The kids were getting off the bus shortly, so we said our good-byes. He walked out the door, and I gasped for air. I felt like I had been punched hard in the gut and didn't really know how to react initially. I poured a big glass of wine and started working on a puzzle since that was calming for me. I don't think he was gone twenty minutes before I started texting him, which continued the rest of the night, back and forth. That could have been the most we had texted back and forth since we started hanging out, and here, we were just friends now. I felt comforted by it. I knew I didn't want him out of my life and felt somewhat at peace and excited to get to know him as a friend. After all, that is always how I started the few real relation-ships in my past and always said I wanted to be friends with someone for a while before dating them so that I knew I could trust they actu-ally liked me for me and not just my looks or body. It sounded like a great concept, and I was confident he would be able to actually see me for who I really was and fall in love with me too.

Although I was initially comforted, I kept drinking that night, and the peace slowly started turning into fear and anxiety. I could no longer concentrate on the puzzle, so I just lay on the couch, lifeless, as the kids watched TV. I got a babysitter and ended up going out with friends and told them the story of Matthew, hoping somehow they would be able to comfort me along with the Pinot Grigio that kept coming. I was temporarily comforted that night but regretted it in the morning of course once my 6:15 a.m. alarm came on to go into work that Friday. I sent a picture to my friend Tom of me looking like death at the front desk—once again a mixture of tiredness, depression, and being hangover. He was nice enough to send me a breakfast sandwich to brighten my mood and help my tummy.

After work and recovering on the couch all day, Erin came over that evening so I could give her the update on Matthew and get her perspective on everything. I told her about our conversation and how we were going to start over and be friends and how I was hopeful we could start dating again in the future. I felt better about it until Marsha, Erin's sister-in-law, came over and made me believe differently. She grew up and knew Matthew even better than Erin and told me that he probably said all that as a way of letting me down without hurting my feelings, and I would not be hearing from him again. "That is just the way Matthew operates," she said. I was shocked. I didn't believe her at first and started arguing with her because he sounded really genuine in the conversation, and I trusted him. As she started talking about ex-girlfriends and his ways from the past, I grew less and less hopeful and started pouring more and more wine. Pretty soon, we had gone through a few bottles of wine between the three of us, and the night was filled with both laughter and tears and not much in between because of the elevated state of our emotions about the death of Marsha's brother, the death of Matthew and I's potential relationship, and all kinds of emotional hurts of the past. I was back to being heartbroken once again.

Matthew and I had previously talked about potentially meeting up with Erin and Kyle and all their friends at a big bonfire event that was going on at the farm across from my neighborhood. Now I was really confused after what Marsha had told me the night before, so I had no idea what was going on. I made plans to go out with Tom and another friend Megan into town that night and possibly meet up with the other guys later on. I was still grieving that night as I told

Tom and Megan the latest update in the saga, and once again, I hit the bar hard in hopes to numb the pain I was still feeling four nights later.

In the midst of them comforting me and us trying to have a good time at the bar, my phone suddenly rang, and it was Matthew calling me. I nearly jumped out of my chair to go answer it, but Tom and Megan screamed "No!" to me and took my phone. They wouldn't let me answer his call. They just had to sit there the last couple of hours listening to my sob story, so I guess I owed it to them not to ditch them to answer this guy's call who hurt me over the last few days. After thorough negotiations back and forth, they realized they were defeated before they even tried, and I was going to call him back.

By the time I called him back, he had already left the bonfire and was heading back home. I was devastated. It was my only chance to see him, and I missed it. I couldn't express my sadness and disappointment over the phone with him because then he would know how much I really did still like him, and that went against what I had just agreed to two days earlier about being friends. I am sure he could tell over the phone though as clearly I had been drinking, and anytime that happened, which was almost every night, my emotions were heightened to a point of being out of control. I lay on the couch inconsolable that night as my friends tried to be there and comfort me for this loss of this guy I barely knew. I didn't understand why I was so destroyed over him; it was such a short time. Was it really possible to be in love with someone that quickly?

After that night, I decided I would try and take the week off from drinking. I went hard all those days in a row, and it only brought on bad decisions, heightened emotions, and drove away a guy I really liked. The following Wednesday was a nice day, and I decided to ask Matthew if he wanted to go for a walk around the lake. I figured it would be a daytime excursion; there would be no drinking involved, and we would be getting exercise all while being able to actually talk and get to know each other as friends. Without the heightened emotions the alcohol brought on, I was once again at peace with trying to pursue a friendship with him.

We walked around all six miles around the lake and had great conversations about our families, work, and life. When we got back our cars, he didn't seem like he wanted to leave me. I played it cool and gave him a quick hug and told him to have a good night. We needed to keep it strictly friends, and I was trying to respect that. At this point, I had forgotten about what Marsha had told me on Friday night. Maybe that was her experience with Matthew, but I trusted him and his intentions at that point and wanting to go for a walk with me further solidified my desire to continue pursuing a friendship with him because I knew he was a good guy and different than anyone I had ever met.

Two days later, I was sitting at work in the morning and was trying to figure out how to formulate a text, asking him to come with me that night to a haunted hayride with a group of friends. While I was editing and reediting, making sure not to sound like I was asking him on a date, I received a text from him first, asking if I wanted to go to a party with him that night with friends in New Jersey. I couldn't help the smile that came wide across my face, thinking about the coincidence there. We were both thinking about each other at the same exact time and wanting to attend events with each other that night. I wondered how long he took to formulate his text.

We decided to go to my haunted hayride first and would go to his friends afterward. We were both proud to share that we hadn't drank all week, but once we got there, we did get drinks. We told each other it was fine. It was hard to act like friends when we were basically out on a date among a group of couples, but I was determined. Things were hard when we were going through the haunted house as I was already terrified with those things. I couldn't help but continue to grab his arm throughout the whole thing. His linen shirt was so soft and his arm underneath was so warm and comforting. Just touching him slightly started bringing back feelings, but I could see that maybe he was having them too.

We left the farm and headed to New Jersey to a house where he only knew the owners and I knew no one. I could tell he was nervous because he didn't really know what to expect, and he knew everyone there would be a lot older than me. It was so cute how he was trying to impress me, not knowing just being in his presence was all I really wanted. With him, we could be by ourselves in the middle of the woods or in the middle of a crowded room, and he would be the only one I would see. Until I started drinking.

He had only experienced me either drunk in a group of people or sober and by ourselves, so he had no idea how shy I was in front of new people without any alcohol. I timidly said hello to his friends then parked myself by the bonfire with a drink in hand. The party dwindled down, and we were left at the bonfire talking with the ex-husband of the woman who was hosting the party with her new fiancé at his former house. The foreshadowing of this circumstance is uncanny, but I cannot say I didn't think about it. Through a series of invasive questions about the dynamic of our "friendship," the man finally asked the obvious question, "Do you love her?" I think the question threw both of us off in his bluntness, but Matthew answered after barely even a pause, "Yes."

I wasn't really sure how to react to this. It had been only a short time we had known each other, and just last week, he sat on my couch, breaking up with me in a romantic way, and now he revealed to a stranger that he loved me.

"So why don't you just be with her?" the stranger asked. I often go back to this night and can't help to think if things would be different if we didn't meet this man, if he didn't ask these questions, and if we didn't go to that party. Would things have turned out differently for us? We thanked the man for talking with us and made our way to Matthew's car. We sat there talking for a few minutes about the conversation that was just held. We each knew what the other was contemplating. "You said you wanted to just be friends, that you were on a certain path, and I do not want to be the one to take you away from that," I told him. There was nothing I wanted more in that moment than to kiss him, but at the same time, I had just been so hurt the week before by him and the changing of his mind about me so quickly. I didn't know what to do but wait for his guidance. Matthew's guidance.

Before I knew it, we leaned in towards each other and kissed. It was soft and gentle, not like the aggressive passionate kisses from nights prior, which were full of sexual tension and lust. It was letting go of all uncertainties of a bruised heart and succumbing to love, or so I thought.

On that fateful Friday, October 25, night, we considered ourselves "dating." We had gone from a drunk connection, to an authentic connection, to ghosting, to being friends, to dating, and not yet a week later, I was now his girlfriend. I had gone from losing the love of my life, to making peace with starting a friendship, to dating again, and to being hesitant to jump into a serious relationship so quickly. I was excited, overwhelmed, yet a little unsure and confused at how it all was taking place.

My marriage lacked passion, now I had it. I always loved roller coasters. Did I now get to experience one pertaining to my life? I was so enamored by him. He was beautiful. We had unbelievable chemistry; the attraction was undeniable. All I wanted to do was be wrapped up in his arms as much as possible all day, every day. He felt warm and soft, and his lips were so smooth and wonderful to kiss and fit with mine perfectly. His simple attire of T-shirts and sweats was perfect to me. When he came back to my house after work, after laboring all day, he had a unique scent of oil, chemicals, and grime, but it was uniquely him, and I loved it. I was always so concerned with hygiene and couldn't stand to be around Eric when he didn't shower, but with Matthew, he could go three days without showering, and I didn't care at all.

He didn't have a college education and didn't make much money, but I didn't care about any of it. I knew he was intelligent and always had so much to offer in a conversation and teach me about. He owned his mistakes of the past and was proud of what he did for work. The passion was always present, and that was what drew me to him. He was hysterical. He could make me laugh even when we would just be sitting and watching a movie. Humor was such an attraction for me. He could talk to anyone. He had a charismatic presence about him that when he spoke to people, you could tell he really listened to them and seemed genuinely interested in what they had to say. I didn't have to babysit or entertain him at group events. He fit right in so that I could be off talking to my girlfriends. I would miss him though after a while and would always glance over to see him with the other men, and it comforted me knowing he was so friendly and just there. It was difficult not to picture our life together in the future.

He was so amazing with my children. He took to them immediately, and even though they were hesitant and unsure of who this new man was in our lives and couldn't really comprehend how to feel about mommy being with someone else besides daddy, he never gave up. He attended every sports game and event and cheered them on; he took care of them when I had too much to drink and wanted to stay late at a neighbor's party. He brought home treats for them after work and played with them in the yard. He immediately took on the role of stepdad when he didn't need to, and there was nothing I loved more than watching him engage with them. He would tell me that even though it was a lifelong dream of his to have children of his own, he would be content loving mine as his own. Just hearing him say that made me want to give him a child, even though I swore I was done.

He also was going to be a good influence on me! D would be proud I found a Christian man. I teetered with the idea of going back to a new type of church here and there but never had that push, so maybe Matthew could be the push I needed. This one I didn't have to wait until marriage to have sexual relations with though, although I wasn't entirely turned off by that idea given my history. Oh, the sex though. How come I didn't feel ashamed afterward with him? How come I felt so safe? I had heard of the concept of two becoming one flesh, but I never understood what that meant. If I had any understanding of what it was, that was how I felt when we were together, not only just physically, but spiritually and emotionally as well. Sometimes, I would cry after, but it was not out of shame as in the past. It was instead an overwhelming feeling of experiencing something I couldn't describe that I could only think comes from God Himself.

CHAPTER 11

The Fall

May 25, 2020

Dear Matthew,

Has it ever occurred to you why I give you this "attitude?" I think you know exactly why I do, and you deflect it back on me because you are really mad at yourself. You look back on all these instances, and I guarantee 90 percent of the time, it was me getting upset with you for smoking, which you yourself want to quit and promised me to! Even yesterday, sure, I was being a baby with Kan Jam but probably because I was already upset with you walking back with everyone after smoking at my daughter's birthday, after you've been saying you'll quit for six months now. Then to blame me for the reason you are smoking? I didn't know you twenty-five years ago. Do not blame me for smoking. I am trying to help you. You made promises to us, and you aren't fulfilling them. You promised you would approach me calmly in the moment if I am doing something that bothers you, yet you haven't tried to do that and saved it for the end after all your anger and drunkenness builds up and then lash out on me when I, too, am beyond drunk. You promised not to call me horrible names and love me for who I am, but instead, it gets worse every time. I, at least, have told you that I would continue to try to fulfill my promises, but it may take time because you are asking me to change who I am and how I have always been. I have been trying, and if you do not see that, then you are blind to anything but your own crazy thoughts. At least I am honest with you and myself and know these changes do not happen overnight. But if you aren't willing to put in the time and effort, then you absolutely do not care. Even still, no one in the world can ever guarantee they will never get mad at someone or give them attitude again. Just like you cannot guarantee you will never have another cigarette again, you will never call me a bad word, or you won't forget to tell me something's bothering you at that time, instead hold it in and yell at me. But if we see the effort in each other, then we can support each other's growth, instead of bringing each other down each time.

You think you do no wrong most of the times and are so fixated on blaming me. You do not see your own imperfections and try to work on those. I am a happy, positive person by nature, but you expect me to act perfectly all the time, and that is just impossible! Especially when I do not get to vent to my boyfriend about it all week because he either isn't talking to me or because if I say I am having an off day, he immediately thinks it's him or someone else I am involved with romantically. In turn, he gets all anxious and worried, and I end up being the one to reassure and comfort him instead of me just needing a hug and support from him.

Do you ever consider my feelings? Did it ever occur to you at all yesterday how awkward it was for *me* to be at my old house for my daughter's birthday and feel like I am sort of hosting, but not really? People asking me where things are and me having to be like "Uh, I don't live here anymore. Ask Eric." How happy people are having a pool to swim in and commenting on how beautiful the yard is and me trying to not be sad about it? Forgive me for getting tipsy and running my mouth. That's how I cope right now, and I know that is a problem, but try having some compassion. Maybe I just wanted you around me and be my partner all night because no matter how weird I felt being there, I could look at you and be happy I am not living there anymore and remember how much better off I am having left. Everyone knows I am a baby and horrible at playing games, but they all love me anyway and accept that about me. You made it quite clear you could not love all sides of me last night, including that bad one, and you certainly didn't do anything to stop yourself from smoking when you knew how much that bothered me on top of everything. Then I get a two-hour lecture about how I do all these things without thinking about the consequences, which is a lot better than you doing them while knowing the consequences ahead of time. Either way, it's wrong of both of us. So why can't we both apologize and come up with a plan to try harder next time? I can't be the only one here. How will you ever understand my perspective and why I do things if you will not listen? You think you know anything that comes out of my mouth is a lie, but you aren't me. You do not know my feelings and my thoughts because you are not me. If I didn't give you attitude or wasn't mad about something but you perceived otherwise, I am not lying if I say you are incorrect.

I don't know anymore. You eventually tell me you don't mean to say these things to me out of anger, but it's hard to ignore. They begin to get ingrained into my head. Nothing is worse than the accusations though. I was literally gone for two minutes to grab sweatpants from my house, and you come running up the street accusing me of being with someone. I put the sweatshirt and sweatpants over my dress out of fear for taking too long at the house, so I was in and out so fast and it still didn't matter. The thoughts of me being with someone else are so mentally destructive for myself because you are the love of my life. There's no one else I even want to look at, let alone be with; and every time you make an accusation, I am forced to have those thoughts in my mind!

*****

Almost instantly, his insecurities started rearing their ugly heads. At first, it was mainly in group settings with my friends. The night after we considered ourselves beginning to date again, I held a Halloween birthday party at my house. Eric was in attendance, and since this was so new, I didn't want to flaunt Matthew off or anything, so we mingled mostly separate the first part of the night;

but as soon as Eric left, I was attached to Matthew. He slept over that night, and I could tell he had something heavy on his mind. "I don't want to be part of a squad," he told me. I wasn't entirely sure what he meant, and after some explanation, I told him he was absolutely the only guy I was talking to. I had told the other three I was talking to that I started dating someone the day after our first real date at his apartment. I was so excited to have him back; the mere thought of anyone else brought me disgust. I did my best to reassure him in the moment, but I could tell he had a heavy heart. Nevertheless, we continued in our bliss.

It seemed anytime we hung out in a group setting, there would always be some single guy he would be worried about and watching me with; and when there weren't any single guys present, he would watch how I was with the other husbands and look for any sort of eye contact or evidence of something more going on than just the friendship we had all developed with each other over the last eight years all raising our children together. If we weren't with my group of friends, we would have been hanging out together at a bar. Then it became a question and subsequently a fight over how I acted toward other male patrons at the bar. Matthew was a smoker, so he would leave me to go smoke several times, and instead of sitting there by myself feeling awkward, I spoke with people around me, whether they were men or women, to occupy my time until he returned. I would apologize continuously, but I didn't even understand why I was apologizing because I was just being myself, who had been a fun and outgoing person. I did enjoy attention, but I didn't know how to behave any differently at that time, especially in the presence of alcohol. To me, it didn't matter; however, Matthew was the only man I ever wanted, so conversing with others in a bar setting just felt normal.

The insecurities spread over to the times when we were doing activities separately. Our first big fight occurred when we had mis-communication over what time I was coming to his apartment after being at a business networking meeting my friend was holding. After I walked in and was questioned as to why I was so late, I made the mistake of telling him he was acting like my ex-husband. He equated that to me calling him abusive because I had told him how our marriage ended. I ended up apologizing and feeling incredibly guilty about it, but in hindsight, he was yelling at me for not being there on time and accusing me of lying, which most would call abusive.

Whether it was going out for a girl's night or simply being at home after working only until lunchtime, there was constant questioning there. Anytime I made plans for a girl's dinner out with the women in my neighborhood, he was sure to start with me about something right as I was all ready to leave. I would get degrading comments such as "Are you going to come right home afterwards, or are you going to make a detour on the way home," with the implication that I would be stopping at a lover's house, even though Erin or someone would be driving all of us together. A few times I had to tell them to come pick me up last because I had been bawling my eyes out and needed time to calm down and redo my makeup to hide the tears. I offered him to track my location at all times on his phone so he could always know where I was, but he refused to do that and said he didn't want to know where I was. I sent him screenshots constantly of group texts among the girls, showing the times we were going and coming back. He ignored my attempts. I offered him to drive me to and from wherever I was headed, but he refused. I did not know what to do to comfort him while I was trying to do my separate thing.

The insecurities even spread into the times when we were together, just the two of us watching TV at home. If I were to get just one text message from anyone, I would get an accusatory "Who's blowing you up?" question as if I was receiving twenty texts in a row. I tried to show him who was texting me and offered my phone so he could see everyone who texted and called me, but he didn't want to see it. I was so enamored by him and so completely in love with him that I chalked it up to a cute type of jealousy. I wasn't hiding anything, so it really didn't matter to me. I kept telling myself it would eventually go away after a few months. He would get to know and trust me more; he would see how in love with him I really was and how I had zero interest with any other man. After all, I couldn't do anything to make Eric jealous of me even when I was purposely trying to flirt with others to get his attention at one point, so it was nice to have a man who "cared" so much about me.

The insecure comments I thought were adorable started turning into fights after only a few weeks. With every fight, however, came a passionate lovemaking session followed by us pouring our hearts out to each other and growing closer. Originally, we would last about three weeks in this obsessive state, then there would be another fight. Most of them stemmed out of his insecurities, his smoking, or my drinking excessively while we were out at a bar or with friends or at a party. It was the only way I knew how to be, using alcohol as a way to escape my insecurities about who I really was to be funny, outgoing, flirty, ditzy, and the center of attention among friends and strangers alike. I didn't drink in middle school or high school, and I was the shy girl in school and, in turn, was bullied and had very few friends. I started drinking alcohol in college to change that, but it wasn't until my father had an affair and abandoned us that I started drinking excessively to mask my pain and put on a completely different identity.

Matthew had already been past that phase of life. He had almost died in a car accident after drunk driving and had slowly turned his life around since then, with regards to drugs and alcohol. Yet he didn't have any compassion, understanding, or even knowledge of why I did it. But neither did I for that fact, and so he took it as me being a promiscuous woman who was trying to get the attention of any guy she could get her hands on.

Over the months, the three weeks of bliss would start to dwindle into two weeks and, eventually, only a week in between fights. Matthew and I had already been staying with each other every night at this point, but if we got in a fight and I needed to be alone, then I would go back to my place if we stayed at his, or I would try to tell him to leave my house. In trying to establish a boundary and give us each space to cool off, the accusations of cheating would only get worse because he would think I was staying with someone else, even if I was on my house phone with him, talking with him the whole time while he was at his apartment. If he was at my house and wouldn't leave, I would drive off to a nearby parking lot to escape the yelling, but instead of cooling down, he thought I was driving to a neighbor's house and having sex with a husband. So I stopped driving off in my car and would instead run out of the house barefooted, many times just in my T-shirt and underwear if I had been in bed, and would go curl up in front of my neighbor's trees. Even half-dressed and no shoes, he still accused me of running to cheat on him.

Many times I didn't even leave the house. I would have to come up with different hiding spots around the house. I stayed curled up behind my air hockey table and a bin of toys for forty minutes while he searched the house calling for me. I heard him searching and felt bad about it. *Wait, why was I feeling bad about it? He had just yelled at me and called me the most awful names. Why am I feeling bad for him now?* I stayed in the garage for two hours once on the floor and even had to urinate so bad I went into a cup so I didn't have to go inside. I laid down behind the seats in my car several times for an hour or so at a time. Each time I was accused of being with someone, even on our property. He never believed where I was. I didn't want to tell him in case I needed those hiding spots again, but at the same time, I couldn't stand him calling me a liar. Not that it did any good for me to tell the truth.

He was incapable of having a rational and calm discussion of whatever it was we were fighting over. Initially, it was legitimate things. I could see how he was bothered by them. Drinking too much, being outgoing, disrespecting him if I didn't get my way—nothing the average guy would probably have been too upset by; but one who had a long life of pain, trauma, and struggle, I could see how he could have gotten upset. I never understood fully because I never meant to cause any harm. I was only being the only person I had known how to be my entire life. But I saw his pain and hurting through every fight, and I empathized with what he was going through, even though it was destroying me.

In his yelling, he started calling me names. It started out with "moron." The very first time he called me that, I didn't know how to react. I was in complete and utter shock and disbelief. I had teased myself for being "blonde" many times, which was my excuse for being a little dumb or ditzy sometimes, but never a moron. The pain of that initial name-calling never really went away. His apology seemed sincere, and I was assured it would never happen again, but that was just the first of many. I thought that was so horrible and degrading, but the rest that followed were far worse and many times over. He called me every name in the book. Ones I cannot write about. The ones that hit me the hardest though were always *liar*, *cheater*, and *whore*. I didn't love myself very much, but the one thing I did always love about myself was that I was an honest person. I always joked that I was incapable of lying, but really, if I tried to, then anyone could tell, so I just didn't bother because that was usually more embarrassing. I was also more faithful to him than anyone I had ever been with. Although I never physically cheated on anyone previously, I almost always did in my mind, which I have come to find out is just as bad. You could not pay me to come up with one name in our entire relationship that I had fantasized about. It just wasn't fair.

After the names, things started getting physical—not with me at first, but with things. One night, he took an axe to the little playhouse he had built for my daughter for her birthday party. He had worked so hard on it for months, and she was so excited to receive it. It was the middle of the night, and he was chopping at this house for the neighborhood to hear. Then he took the axe to the flooring he had fixed in the basement. Anything he had worked on or fixed in the house was destroyed that night. From that day on, I could not recall another project he helped out with around the house.

The yelling got louder and louder overtime, and eventually, things turned physical with me. I wasn't as scared as I was absolutely desperate. The only things I knew how to do were either yell back in defense of whatever he was calling me—saying, "I am not a liar," or "I am not a cheater"—run away, or lock myself in the bedroom or bathroom. Once again, I was the scared little six-year-old hiding from my mother in my closet. Except now, I was thirty-five, and I was up against a man with a temper.

None of my survival methods seemed to work with him. If I tried yelling back at him and got in his face, then he would push me down. The first time it was off my deck. There was no railing on the deck as it was just a three-foot drop with large bushes right off it. I went clear over the bushes and landed flat on my back and head. I couldn't breathe for what seemed like a lifetime but was probably only about twenty seconds. I also couldn't move. Was I paralyzed? My head hurt so much instantly. He quickly ran down to check on me. I could hear the panic in his voice. It took me several minutes to be able to move and be helped up to my feet. Once he got me to a couch, which even felt excruciating, he started yelling that he couldn't do this anymore and that he could not end up in jail. Through all my pain, I was most hurt from him threatening to leave. My neck, spine, and lower back will never be fully recovered from the fall, but I will forever be thankful that I was not paralyzed that day. I lied to the doctors, my friends, and my family about what happened. It's funny how he always accused me of lying to him when I felt I needed to lie about him to everyone else.

We made up and continued on, but that was not enough to cause him to want to change. I was still pushed several more times after that. One time, my head went through a wall, and when weeks went by without him fixing it, I needed to patch up my own head hole because it hurt every time I looked at it. Other times, my knees and elbows hit the hardwood floors or a piece of furniture on my way down with such force that the bruising remained for weeks. When I was on the ground, he mocked me for crying out in pain, bullying me to get up off the ground as if I were exaggerating the fall on purpose. I tried mocking him one time as he was yelling at me in bed, thinking maybe he would get a taste of what it felt like, but then he dumped an entire bowl of ravioli and red sauce over my head. I never did that again.

If I ran away, he would start yelling outside for the neighbors to hear, and then accuse me of cheating. If I tried locking myself in the bedroom or bathroom, he would knock the doors down, and then I'd be out $60 for a new door and all the work of painting, sanding, cutting, and hanging a new one. I went through four doors. Nothing I ever tried worked. I started praying as a last resort. It felt like God had abandoned me. I was a good person, all I wanted was to love and be loved. Why did I deserve this treatment?

I did slap Matthew twice during our relationship. He would grab onto my thighs when we would be intimate with each other, and days later, when the bruises would show up, he would accuse me of having someone else give me fingerprint bruises on my thighs and bottom. That was a frequent accusation from him. I also get jumped on by about forty dogs a day, so bruises are completely normal for me. The way he accused me one time was so disgusting I couldn't help myself and slapped him. The other time was when he called me an awful degrading name I didn't know how to respond, and that was my best defense in the moment. I also did throw my phone at him once when he was accusing me of cheating again, and I told him he can have my phone and look all through it because I wasn't hiding anything. I guess you can say I was also physically abusive. I asked for forgiveness, not that I was getting any help from God to prevent me from letting my anger get that bad. I hated who I turned into during these times of absolute desperation. I had spent an entire year in therapy for my anger issues after college, in dealing with my father, and just like that, all that work had begun to unravel in my desperate attempts to protect myself.

If I was lucky enough to sneak back in the house after running away and him being asleep in the family room, I would go right up to bed and have some peace. But before I knew it, the bedroom light would come flashing on, and the covers were torn off of me, and the yelling would continue. I tried to bury my head so far into my pillow or into a corner, thinking maybe I could melt into them and disappear, but he was always right there at my ear. I would be so exhausted sometimes I didn't even have the strength to argue. Sometimes, I couldn't handle it anymore and just told him that he was right. I was a cheater and a liar. I had tried everything else. Why not try giving in to him? Almost immediately, a voice would say, "No! Do not succumb to the accusations, then you would actually be what he is accusing you of, which is what he ultimately wants! He wants to force you into behaving the way that he is accusing you of behaving so that he can have his excuse to be right and leave the relationship!" So I would immediately recant, and we would be back to square one.

I remember one time he was really tired and wanted to go to bed before me. I wasn't quite ready yet, so I asked to stay in the family room and continue watching my show, and I would be up in a little while. I went upstairs maybe half an hour later, but sometime later, he woke up and flipped out, wondering where I had been and who I had been with. From then on, he would stay up late on the couch downstairs watching TV, eating his bags of chips, and I would head up to bed because it was too late for me, and he would end up falling asleep down there. Each night, I would wake up at some point, hearing the rumbling of the television still on, and I would go downstairs to shut it off. Initially, I would wake him up to come to bed, but when he wondered why I was still awake in an accusatory tone, I eventually just left him down there to sleep.

I am naturally a poor sleeper who typically wakes up around 3:00 a.m. most nights to go to the bathroom or just lay awake with hundreds of thoughts racing through my mind. I remember telling him I would wake up in the middle of the night, and from then on, almost every night was a struggle when he was in bed with me. He swore I would wake up, go downstairs, and have sex with someone in our family room. Right there, in the house where he was asleep upstairs, along with my two children. I knew he already thought I was a sick person to cheat on him anyway, but to bring someone into our house to do it? I knew something was seriously wrong. From that point on, I started taking sleeping pills again to try and sleep through the night. If I did wake up and had to go to the bathroom or get a drink of water from downstairs, I knew I couldn't. If he woke up as I was getting back into bed, it would be over. I fought the need to do these things out of fear and subsequently suffered because of it. Anything I could possibly do to prevent him from getting upset and a fight starting, I tried.

I typically only worked until lunchtime so I would come home and clean the house, go for a walk, or complete chores for a couple hours until it was time for both him and the kids to get home from their days. I would take a shower before they got home so I could spend time with them when they got home and also to be clean for the rest of the night. I did work with dogs all day, so I felt gross anyway and always liked showering in the afternoon. This turned into a problem eventually too as he became worried that I was washing off sex from someone that was with me right before he got home. I made the mistake of asking him to let me know what time he was leaving work each day so I could have a heads-up, and to him, that meant so I could be with someone and quickly get them out of the house and then shower before he got home. So instead of respecting my wishes, he wouldn't let me know when he was on his way home and would show up at random times—sometimes very early, like he was trying to catch me in the act. He never did because there was nothing to catch. Yet he still did not trust me. I was now scared to even shower.

When we weren't fighting, things were amazingly perfect. I couldn't ever take my eyes off him with the biggest smile on my face, completely infatuated with every inch of his body, his beautiful brown eyes, and the passion in his voice when he spoke about something that interested him. He was so charismatic and funny; he always had me laughing when I wasn't crying. When we made love, it was like something I had never felt before. It felt out of this world, biblical to me. It felt like we were really two becoming one flesh in every sense. I felt safe, wanted, attractive, and loved. I held onto all these things through the worst of times. When I had nearly given up, I clung to the happy times. They still outweighed the bad times, right? I clung to the man I knew he was underneath all the pain that engulfed him. The passionate, emotional, loyal, loving man underneath the constant struggle to fight what was in his DNA that he could never face. I clung to this hope when everyone around me was telling me to get out.

This roller coaster of emotions continued throughout the relationship. A little over a year into our relationship, things started going even more downhill as the fights were every few days and lasted for even longer and for reasons that seemed to be out of nowhere. Every other time I had upset him, I felt I had "learned my lesson" and did everything I could to "behave" as perfectly as possible so I knew they were no longer my issues. I started forgetting what we were even fighting about at this point, but it always seemed like the same accusatory cheating or if he didn't like some type of attitude I had about something. My praying got more frequent, and they were focused on Matthew, solely for him to get the help he needed; however, I still wasn't seeing any change, and I felt more and more hopeless.

Since God was not helping me and I was so desperate for answers, one awful night, I reached out to his ex-girlfriend, asking how he behaved with her. Without even asking any specific questions, she wrote me back a long text about many of the behaviors he did, and I became sick to my stomach as my worst fears were confirmed about the love of my life as the behaviors were exactly the same. However, she got out before it got physical. She was still struggling with the pain of being a victim of verbal and emotional abuse all this time later. Was that going to be me? *No, he loved me. He wanted to marry me. He would change for me!* I felt so desperate and helpless, I then reached out to his mother, and she insisted his father come over that night, which happened to be my birthday, to talk to him. It was the worst birthday of my entire life. Me, who's birthday is my favorite day of the year.

I was overcome with anxiety as I paced back and forth, waiting for his dad to get there and for Matthew to get home from work. He walked in what seemed like forever later with flowers and balloons. Immediately, my stomach dropped, and I felt guilty. What had I done? Was he trying to make up with me and do something sweet? How could I have called his mother? Now his father was on his way over to essentially back him into a corner and make him get help, and he was going to be so angry.

The talk didn't go well. Matthew didn't respond well and exposed me for things in front of his father, instead of taking responsibility for anything that was wrong with him. This was all ironic because his ex-girlfriend had just told me that morning that she, too, had reached out to his mom several times and had gotten the same response from her, which was to leave Matthew, but she would send her husband over to talk to him, and it never did anything. Why was I so blind thinking anything I did would have a different outcome? He loved me more than her; he wanted to try and be better, right?

My brother also came over that night because he was worried that I had canceled my birthday dinner with the family, and he tried talking with Matthew as well. I had learned that night that you cannot rationalize with an irrational person, and once again, I had just made matters worse. I didn't think we would recover after that night because he knew now that he was exposed. Somehow, we did. I ended up apologizing for everything, and I ended up agreeing to go to alcohol-addiction counseling after he told his dad and my brother how my drinking was to blame for so many of our fights. The whole next day, I called addiction centers. *Wait a minute…this intervention was for him. How did I end up taking blame and agreeing to go get help for something when he hadn't agreed to changing anything about himself?*

The praying got more frequent as the bad times started getting more frequent. I never once prayed for me though. I thought it was just him that needed the help. Nothing was getting better though. In fact, they were getting worse. The jealousy, the accusations, the mistreatment, the length of the silence that followed the fights—it all was getting worse.

CHAPTER 12

A Second Chance

April 29, 2021

I had a horrible day at work. All I wanted to do was call Matthew to vent, but he made it clear I could not vent to him from the other night and Saturday in the car. He asked if I wanted to talk about it when I came upstairs crying, and I said no. Instead of listening to me, he asked why I didn't want to talk about it, and I asked, "Are you serious?" referring to the previous nights when he told me he was not my counselor or psychologist. His comforting lasted about thirty seconds before he flipped out on me and told me that was not what he said. Then it proceeded on and on, and we have yet another example of how he made me feel worse instead of better.

Later on, he was in the guest bathroom from 8:15 to 8:48 p.m. I had gone to bed as soon as the kids went down because I was so upset. Around eight forty-five, I heard some thumps, so I walked out, and he was still in the bathroom. I knocked and asked if he was okay. He gave me the nastiest look and said, "What? Because I am in the shower?" I told him I heard two thumps, and he said, "The only noise you heard was you knocking." Was I going crazy? Minutes later, he said the thumps were coming from downstairs (so he did hear them too?), and it was me coming up the stairs. Obviously, I had been in bed the whole time, and I wasn't coming up the stairs;

and even if I was, why would I ask him what my own thumps were? He was so awful, just for me caring if he fell in the shower or something. All I want is for him to show me he cares for me and about me, including me feelings, and he doesn't. He does the opposite. But anytime I try and show him I care, or offer him help, he gets mad at me.

He gets so mad at me and ends up yelling at me like a parent-child relationship, instead of approaching and talking to me with respect and love. It escalates really quick as I start crying because he says then I am making him out to be the bad guy and I am playing victim. Then I finally get mad as he pushes and pushes and I freak out, and he calls me crazy and possessed.

Most of the times he gets mad at me are because he has spoken to me in a rude or condescending sort of way, and either I get hurt from it or I "give attitude" back in response, and he forgets or doesn't realize why I am doing that. Or if I am bothered by his smoking or taking a long time to get ready to leave somewhere.

He has had an entire lifestyle change and keeps changing different things and has high expectations of me adapting right away and accepting it without feelings, and when I can't do that, he gets mad. I usually adapt within a few days, but that is not quick enough for him.

- No sex, touch or kissing
- Not sleeping with me in bed
- Having all his belongings in the garage except for the things kept in the dining room
- Not smoking weed, now not drinking, but still smoking cigarettes—the one thing I actually wanted him to give up
- Not caring about my feelings or anything and expecting me not to have them
- Not hanging out with friends or neighbors at houses
- Not wanting to go out to dinner much, or any date really
- Devoting any extra time that could be spent with me alone or work on house projects to others

I have an extremely difficult time talking to him and being open about my feelings or things that bother me because he has made it clear he does not care about my feelings. He interrupts me frequently and has a way of making it about him and proving a point, offering unsolicited advice, which ultimately makes me more upset than where I started and, in turn, causes a fight. I have to tiptoe around him because I am so scared anything I say could potentially set him off, or how I say it even. Whether it has anything to do with him or not, like if I am having a bad day, any tone I use will set him off or offend him. The uncertainty of what our relationship will look like and what I can expect out of him has been weighing heavily on my heart. Will I be alone at every social event? Will we not be able to talk anymore about work, feelings, the future, making plans, or religion? Can I drink in front of him? Will we be able to go out to dinners? Can I have parties at our house and count on him to stay, or will he leave those nights? What are we left with besides things with the kids? Does he love me without them? Or does he only love them?

*****

Matthew seemed to have a wake-up call with the Lord one day after two back-to-back health struggles. I think he realized for a brief moment in time that I actually did love and care about him because we had, of course, been in a fight, but I put all that aside to care for him. He realized God was clearly trying to pull him back to his faith, which he had basically abandoned early on in our relationship because of the powers of the flesh, the world, and the devil. We started going back to the church he had been part of before he met me and where he had taken me once in the beginning of our relationship but stopped because he just assumed I didn't want to be there, and I never spoke up to let him know otherwise.

All of a sudden, he seemed to have a new attitude on life and a new passion, and I was feeling hopeful. We were getting along again for a little while, and although he started throwing scripture into everything and preaching down my throat until I felt overwhelmed, I didn't mind too much because he was treating me better. It did become overwhelming at times because he wanted so badly for me to share in what he was going through. He failed to take the time to figure out the best way to go about doing that so that I would be open and understanding to it all because Matthew seemed to believe, as with everything else, that his way was the right way.

The next thing he told me was he no longer wanted to put himself in social situations with my friends, or even strangers, by going out to dinner with just the two of us. Most of these situations involved drinking, and he didn't want to be any part of it. This was something that was weekly, or even twice weekly, in our neighborhood between birthday parties, game nights, or playdates. I had done these events solo before, but I actually wanted to have Matthew there with me, even though so many fights had started because of them before. I failed to see that though and only saw our brilliant future of not fighting after he changed and could be normal around me and everyone else.

A few days later, he told me that he was going to go to men's Bible study on Monday nights, followed by practicing soccer with his nephew Tuesday and Thursday nights, something else another night, and then church and classes every Sunday—no matter what plans we had already had as we were approaching spring and summer. As someone who never had any plans each night to having almost every night filled up with something that didn't include me, this came as a big shock to me. That mixed with not wanting to hang out with my friends anymore was a huge blow to me. We already didn't do much because we were usually fighting, so what would we be left with? Being the impulsive emotional person I am, I went with the first feelings that popped up, which were of hurt, betrayal, and abandonment that he didn't want to spend time with me anymore and I complained. Instead of being compassionate and hearing out my feelings, he started arguing right back, and now I was a selfish brat for complaining about it.

After sleeping on it, I realized if it was going to make him a better person and treat me better, I decided I was going to be fine with it, and we would figure it out. Maybe if he had these things to do on these nights, then he wouldn't give me a hard time about going out with girlfriends or hanging out with neighbors by myself since he no longer wanted to be part of it. I came to terms with it the next day. I didn't have a choice really; he was going to do it no matter what, and if I wanted him to stay with me, then I had to be on board.

Once that settled in, he brought up the next change. Next, he started preaching about Paul's letter to the Corinthians and played the chapters for me on the Bible app. Not really sure what he was getting at, I hesitantly asked what he was trying to tell me. Now it was abstinence. "You want to be abstinent now?" I couldn't hide my dropped jaw and wide eyes as I stared at him in disbelief. This was a guy who wanted to make love three times a day every day—morning, noon, and night—and now he wanted to be abstinent?

"What does that entail exactly? No sex?"

"Well, kissing leads to sex, so really we shouldn't be doing anything."

How could we have a relationship without even kissing? Wouldn't that just make us friends? The no-kissing rule then turned into not even hugging or touching because any touch of my body, and he would want to do more, and since he couldn't control himself, I had to suffer. I was fine without the sex, but I needed affection at least. His hugs were the absolute best thing in my life and were what drove me to feel safe and comforted by him. This wasn't fair. Our whole relationship he complained about me making decisions without him, and now that's all our life had become. He was making one decision after another without even talking with me about it and just dictating that this is what he would be doing and just expecting me to go along with everything without any question or input. I once again felt like the child in our relationship and just had to go along with everything he said, even though he was taking away the one thing that provided me safety, comfort, and affection. We fought again that night over it, but after sleeping on it, I thought to myself, *If this will make him treat me better, then I am all for it. I am willing to do anything at this point for this man and our relationship.*

I was so desperate, the next day, I could only think of one person to reach out to who may understand where Matthew was coming from with all this, and I really wanted to understand. I hadn't spoken to him in almost two years since I didn't feel comfortable talking to any guys while I was with Matthew, but I didn't know where else to turn. I sent a text to D, asking if we could talk. I told him about my situation and Matthew wanting to become abstinent now and asked him about his commitment to save himself for marriage. We talked for an hour, speaking about scripture, his beliefs, and where we were each at in our relationships. I felt better after talking things through and was confident that I could move forward with this. D explained to me if a man was willing to make this commitment to God, then he was a man worth keeping. I listened.

I had to stop Matthew the first few times he started losing control of himself, reminding him of what he had asked me for. Just as he had asked to step back and be friends after we had first met, I wanted to respect these wishes as well. It was really hard because he constantly commented on how I looked, stared at me with those piercing eyes up and down my body, and if we did hug, then he couldn't let go. After the third night, I, too, caved into my own desires, could no longer say no, and we made love. The next day, he was on his knees, crying in repentance, pushed me away, and I, in turn, felt like a cheap whore born from the devil himself. It was more degrading than being raped in a parking lot outside a restaurant two years prior. I decided I was not going to be doing that anymore for my own good!

The abstinence soon turned into not sleeping in the same bed together. Slowly, we went from a romantic couple to roommates: me in our room and him on the family room couch. However, I did not receive any of the benefits of him being a boyfriend, especially since he still came in the room at 4:30 a.m. to get ready for work. If he wasn't going to be sleeping in bed with me, at least spare me from the early morning wake-up call and let me sleep in. However, we were on week two of no serious fights, so I was willing to keep going on with it.

Even with all the new concessions I was making in our relationship, his newfound faith back in God brought on a new set of problems and anger. All of a sudden, I wasn't a good enough Christian. I didn't understand or support what he needed to do. I didn't read the Bible enough, the self-help books I had been reading were destructive and worldly, and I was terrible because I was of the world and loved worldly things because I enjoyed hanging out with my friends, who also were not good enough Christians or nonbelievers. I enjoyed having fun, and a trait I once thought was good about myself became a deal breaker. All of a sudden, he would use it against me and mock me in a nasty tone, saying, "You just want to have fun"; like that was such a bad thing. Was I not supposed to have fun in life? Why would I be drawn to Christianity like he was trying to push on me if I couldn't have fun anymore? Was me having fun hurting God in some way or other people? I didn't understand.

The music I listened to was now being trash-talked. Songs would come on that he would bash, so I would have to change them right away. One of the qualities he said he loved about me in the beginning of our relationship was how much he loved how I always had music on in the house. This quickly became another fight. He would come in the house after work, and if a song happened to be playing that resonated with him in any negative way, he would accuse me of putting it on as he was pulling in so he would get a hint of some kind when he walked in. He actually thought I would wait by the window until he came home and would change the song to play to him, as if I wanted to get yelled at by his reaction in some way. Most of the time, it was the radio and I had no control whatsoever as to what was playing. What used to bring me joy now just brought on fears and anxieties over what song would play next, so I stopped playing music in the house. I lost another part of myself that others had loved.

Spring came, and Matthew told me he wanted to get baptized at the church. "Weren't you already baptized?" I asked.

"That was as an infant. I had no control over that. This is as an adult, and I want to make my own decision to walk with Christ."

I didn't understand it, but at this point, nothing he could tell me would come as a shock as everything the last few weeks had brought on. He asked me to join him at baptism class one Sunday, and reluctantly, I did. It was the last place I wanted to be, but I sat there and listened to everyone's stories and why they were there. *I was already baptized*, I kept saying to myself. *Why would I ever want to do it again?*

After baptism class, he asked me to stick around for a starter's class for new believers in Christ to learn about the faith. I couldn't believe I was going to be hanging around for yet another hour at church, but I agreed again. I wanted to be supportive of what he was going through, even though I certainly didn't understand it, and it was the last place I wanted to be. Surprisingly, the class piqued my interest. I had a lot of questions, and it seemed like everyone else had similar ones. Maybe I wasn't alone? As everyone was going around talking, I really empathized with one of the women there who was an addict and came from a family of addicts and was struggling with forgiveness and how to go about living life really. I contributed to the conversation and wanted so badly to help her. Maybe this Christianity thing wasn't so bad after all.

Throughout my time with Matthew, I was doing a lot of soul-searching and self-help. I realized my prayers for him were not working, and any efforts I had made failed, so I had no choice but to try and change myself and my thinking, and maybe that would save our relationship. I had discovered that I was codependent and started researching and reading up on that. I offered whatever advice to this woman I could muster up, which was probably me acting in codependency at the time; but nevertheless, I actually felt good about attending the class. If I couldn't help Matthew, maybe I could help someone else.

We made an honest effort to go to church each week, even if we had been fighting the night before. Although it started out as something I wanted to do for him, I eventually started enjoying the sermons and found myself wanting to go, but only if it was convenient and we didn't have any other plans of course. The fights continued though. When we made it to church, we would usually forget about them for the time being and come back together. If he was too upset to go, however, and I wanted to go, he would become very angry, and another fight would ensue. One morning, I left to go, and he called me, telling me that he refused to let the dog back inside after potty, and if I wanted him back inside, I would have to turn around and come back. The thoughts of my geriatric deaf-and-blind dog outside by himself without a fence, wandering into the streets as he often did, filled my mind, and I begged for him to let him in over the phone, and he refused. I was on my way to church on my own accord for the first time in my entire life, and I had to turn around to save my dog's life. Why was God allowing that?

His mind was so dead set on this new path, yet I wasn't reaping any benefits of it, and it certainly didn't seem like he was either. It seemed like the closer he tried getting to God, the greater his struggle became, and in turn, the angrier he would get at me. I could tell there was constant turmoil going on inside of him, and I wanted desperately for him to feel better, but I didn't know what to do. I didn't know much about Christianity at that point, but I didn't think Christians were supposed to be filled with so much hatred and anger. While the physical abuse subsided, the emotional and verbal were still present and worse than ever now as the new-believer honeymoon phase quickly ended with him.

It seemed like everything I tried talking to him about was turned around into a lesson I needed to learn, and now he was more like a strict yet absent parent I was living with than a roommate or boyfriend. One afternoon, I tried talking about how I was stressed at work because an employee who was "on call" couldn't come in when we needed her, and I didn't do anything to penalize her even though I had told her the day before we actually didn't need her, so she went forward with making plans. I was already upset with myself with how I handled it and was not looking for a lecture, just simply needing to vent. Because he was learning how to "speak the truth in love," he no longer wanted to be "my therapist," and instead, he lectured me within this parent-child dynamic, where I was the constantly-disciplined child who could never do anything right. Except his lectures were not given in a loving way but a yelling way that caused me to feel belittled, stupid, and worthless. His intentions seemed well in hindsight, but the vessel to get there seemed like pure hatred. I was once again back to my childhood, desperate for a nurturing and loving environment, but instead walking on eggshells, just desperate for love and acceptance.

CHAPTER 13

The End of the Road

June 19, 2021

I don't even know where to start tonight. Let's start from now and go backward to yesterday or really Tuesday for that matter. I just basically had an intervention with my family. "I would be honored if you would take me as I am." That is the line I keep listening to since on my way back from Belmar. What a concept. Taking me as I am. It's a reoccurring theme in love stories. Accept me for who I am—the good, bad, and the ugly. That is all I want. So many people love me for who I am. Why can't Matthew? My family brought this up tonight coincidentally after I heard it twice and cried twice on the way home today.

I wish I had a recording of the conversation, because of course, I'll forget it all. They asked why I wasn't at the shore, so I explained it was because he asked me if I wanted the windows closed, so I went upstairs and closed the bedroom window, but it reeked of smoke. I simply asked him if he smoked in the bedroom. It was that powerful. From there, we didn't go because "I attacked him," because it was such a horrible thing to have the nerve to ask if he had the nerve to smoke in the house. My mom had plenty to say about him right off the bat. Ron just wanted me to be happy, and they all "just want me to be able to be myself," and they are afraid I am losing the "bright, sunny, motivated, independent, positive, fun person they have known to be for thirty-six years"!

This one hits me the hardest. My mom said, "He's destroyed you. Look at you. You are destroyed and a shell of the woman you once were." I held it together as best I could all day. I can't stop crying now. I know I need to journal, but I can't even write the words. He doesn't compromise. He never meets me halfway. I always compromise to him. It's his way or no way. This is what my family notices! Not even what I tell them! Gosh, if they even knew the half of it. What do I do now? It's clearly an unhealthy relationship. He *needs* to get help. He must have a mental illness. I want him so bad, but is that really the best thing for either of us? Ultimately, I want to see him flourish. I know he can! I'd rather it happen with me, but it doesn't seem like it will happen like this unless he gets serious help, and that won't happen if he can't admit to his problems. If he can't admit to his problems and get help for them, then he's better off not in a relationship, and it's extremely difficult to come to terms with that when I want him to be my partner more than anything in the world. It just sucks. I know the right answer, but it's not the one I want, so it's hard to admit to. I can't even write anymore about this weekend. It just hurts too much.

*****

By the time summer hit, it seemed like we were just going through the motions of being in a relationship but really not. He went from wanting to marry me to being a roommate, to trying to be my father, to just someone who occupied a room in my house I couldn't even talk to anymore. I am not sure what he was trying to hold onto, but it seemed to me that he would try to come up with any excuse to fight and want to leave me. Many times, he would pack up all his belongings into bins and move them to the garage. He abandoned me over and over, and each time, I was left completely isolated, desolated, and not knowing what to do or what to say, just like that time my dad left me all alone on our living-room floor. I had to relive that moment over and over with Matthew, and each time, I was desperate for a different outcome. All I knew is that I wanted to be with him, but I didn't know how. I had completely lost myself in trying to make him happy, and it seemed like the harder I tried, the more I pushed him away.

By this point, we were in a fight more than we were happy. I couldn't talk to friends or family anymore because I knew their opinions, and they no longer wanted to hear my excuses for him. We were supposed to go on vacation with the whole family in July, but we were fighting a lot up until then. On the morning of departure, I tried to make amends and got up really early and ran to the store to get him coffee and sugar so he would have it when he woke up, but I was only accused of going to see someone else that morning. Instead of listening to him badger me during the car ride, I put my headphones in and listened to music for the car ride, so no fights would start in front of the kids. At one point, he was arguing with my daughter, so I had to take them out, and then it started. He started complaining that I didn't pack him beer, even though I had packed everything for everyone that entire week, including the car, and had gone out that morning to get coffee. But it wasn't enough as usual, and he found a place to complain that I did not pack him beer. I didn't even think he was drinking at that point since he was so back and forth about it, so I just figured he could get some down there if he wanted it.

A fight ensued, and soon enough, he stopped the car in the middle of the highway and got out and started walking, leaving me in the passenger seat and the terrified kids in the back seats crying, wondering what was going on. My son, who can only say a few phrases we can understand since he is mostly nonverbal, tearfully said, "Bye, Matthew." It was a dreadful day, and two and a half hours of smooth riding down to Delaware turned into six hours in the car of back and forth, back and forth, to different parts of Delaware and Maryland, waiting for Matthew to exercise his power and control over me. Telling me he was getting a rental car and going home but then calling me forty minutes later, yelling at me for not coming back for him. Then I would turn around, and he would yell at me to not bother, so I listened to that, only to have him call back and yell again for not coming back for him; the kids, a witness to all of it.

After an entire wasted day, we got to the house with my family and ended up having the most perfect week together on vacation. I wasn't even sure what the point of that whole fight even was. It took all about two minutes to run into the package store, which was right on the way to the house for him to get his beer. Once we met up with my family and the trip officially restarted, he was calm, helpful, sweet, caring, fun, amazing with the kids, affectionate toward me, and we were back to having deep conversations throughout the week. I kept telling him there was no reason we could not be like this when we were back home. *Why couldn't every day feel like a vacation for us? Look how happy we were.* I was hopeful this was a turning point in our relationship. It wasn't until we were on our way back and we crossed the border into Pennsylvania that the questions started, the uneasiness started, the fears crept in, and his anxiety became my anxiety.

We never recovered after that week. The day we got back, I sensed his insecurities, and I reverted back to walking on eggshells. Two days later, I had plans with my two girlfriends from high school, and he couldn't even function that afternoon. I again offered my phone, my GPS location, and I asked him to drive me there and pick me up so he could meet them—anything I could think of. He curled up in a ball in bed and went to sleep. I don't remember a good day after that week in July. I went through the motions. I waited for him to love me again. I waited for him to change, to get help, to have some revelation that it wasn't me who was such a bad guy, that I really did love him and mean well. I started praying for myself. I begged for help, guidance, and direction.

I eventually started playing my music again. I needed something to live for, to keep me distracted, to relate to. My boyfriend wasn't talking with me, so let me find solace in singing these songs to myself. This time, I was more conscience of what stations I had on. He stopped helping me with things around the house. It was home from work, then right to the couch to watch television. I was at a stalemate because I didn't want to nag him, but if I would ask, he wouldn't do the things I asked. I gave him a chance, months even sometimes, and when I couldn't wait anymore, I just did the things myself. When I did, I was accused of having another man come in and do them for me, even though I was so proud I did them myself. I didn't give him any problems about it. I just went ahead and did it. I wasn't rude or mean about him not helping me, but empowered that I could do the things myself. That feeling was quickly diminished when I was made to feel like a prostitute for giving my body away to someone in exchange for installing a water softener or installing a door that he had broken down months prior.

The mudroom addition had been finished, but we had to do the floor ourselves. He said he would help me but wanted to put it off several days because he was tired from work. I decided I would try tiling the floor and painting it myself over several days since I had the time and I wanted it done. He also didn't really seem to have interest in helping, so I didn't want to push it. My phone was literally on the charger in the other room, and he stormed in and yelled that I had put a song on while he was pulling up to the house after work that was bashing him. Somehow he thought I telepathically changed the song when he pulled up. The next day, he came storming in and asked if I had just turned the music on when he pulled in (because there was a break in songs at the exact second he walked into the garage). I asked why I would have had it off while I was home alone and then all of a sudden turn it on when he pulled in. If anything, it would have been the opposite for fear a song came on that he couldn't handle hearing because he knew the song was about him after all. No matter what was going on, there was something he needed to pick a fight with me about.

One night, I was painting the mudroom, and he complained about whatever genre of music I was playing that night, so I put on my hip-hop dancing music instead, and he accused me of being with someone in the mudroom while he was right inside and somehow "getting down" with them to this music. He was in the living room and thought someone was with me thirty feet away in the mudroom. He came over at one point and smacked me so hard in the butt and said, "That ass," in his sleezy pretend hip-hop voice. It was in that moment I realized I would no longer take his abuse. I looked at him straight in the eyes, stood tall, tried to hold back my tears for a good three seconds, then turned around and silently went back to my work. I didn't say a word or try and fight back. I think we both knew it was over in that moment.

I don't remember talking much over the coming week, but I knew I had to allow him to be the one to make the decision to leave, so I was just waiting. I no longer wanted to try and be in control. I realized I hadn't been the whole time, even though I was constantly accused of being so, and wanting that just always made things worse and more painful for both of us. If I tried to tell him to leave, I don't know what would have happened, but I knew it would not have gone well. I knew there would be backlash, accusations, and destruction. His loss of control over me may have caused more pain for me; we would have been enemies, and I did not want that for us or my children.

The thought of failure engulfed me. I had failed as a child to gain acceptance and emotional connections to my parents. Each relationship since has been my chance to go back to that "familiar home" and fix what I was lacking then, and those were failures. This was the closest one to home because I loved him the most, and he was most like my mother. As emotionally and physically destructive as it was, it was the most familiar, and it was my final chance to fix everything so I could finally complete my life's work and live happily ever after. I tried so hard, offered everything I had, offered any and all kinds of solutions, pulled out all the stops, and it still wasn't good enough. I realized I was codependent, and my addiction to love and other's approval was just as bad as anything Matthew was dealing with.

CHAPTER 14

Finding My Identity

August 19, 2021

I've got nothing left. So much has happened. So much was said. I've reached that point everyone keeps talking about. I don't think I can forgive anymore. I can't forgive what was said on Tuesday. Today. I can't do it anymore. I can't hear the words liar, cheater, or scumbag anymore. I can't be made out to be the selfish one, the lying one, when it is him. I've got nothing left. I can't even write anything tonight. All of my being is used up. It's all hopeless. I am destroyed. God answered my ultimate prayer when Matthew defaced the prayer card I lovingly wrote out for him. He made my decision. That is what I was waiting for, I guess. Not what I wanted, but at least it's made. God knows what is right, and I just need to trust Him at this point. What else can I do? I've got nothing else left.

*****

One day in August, I found myself at church, even though Matthew had not wanted to come that day. Things were so bad between us, but I let him know I was going because there was a premarital counseling class afterward we were supposed to attend together, but he never responded, so I decided to go anyway in hopes he would still show up. I was working that morning and decided to just go directly on my own. The sermon was done by someone new this time. It was refreshing. The verse he focused on was 1 Corinthians 9:19–23 (ESV).

> For though I am free from all, I have made myself a servant to all, that I might win more of them. To the Jews I became as a Jew, in order to win Jews. To those under the law I became as one under the law [though not being myself under the law] that I might win those under the law. To those outside the law I became as one outside the law [not being outside the law of God but under the law of Christ] that I might win those outside the law. To the weak I became weak, that I might win the weak. I have become all things to all people, that by all means I might save some. I do it all for the sake of the gospel, that I may share with them in its blessings.

I didn't really know what it's full meaning would be to me until the future, but I felt compelled to write it down. Over the last few months, Matthew had made it a point to tell me how we shouldn't hang out with nonbelievers anymore, that anyone I was friends with was of this world, and he no longer wanted them in our lives. To me, this passage seemed to be saying we should adapt ourselves to certain people and situations so that we can bring Christ to them. Maybe this was to be my gift. I felt the wheels began to turn rapidly in my mind as this passage began to speak to me, and I had a new sense of hope. It wasn't in our relationship as I had previously tried to relate everything back to, but it was in me. It was an unfamiliar feeling, but a good one. We were asked to stand after the sermon so the church band could play one final song at the end. It was one that sounded familiar, and as I looked up at the screen to read the words, all of a sudden, it hit me through the simple yet beautiful lyrics in a song they were playing. God wasn't just my friend or higher power, he wasn't just Jesus's father, no, He was mine too! I was his *child*!

Tears came pouring out immediately as this realization came to me. He was speaking to me through song that day because that is the only way He knew I would listen, that's all I ever listened to. Music was everything to me. I could relate to almost any song out there to suit every type of emotion or situation I was in at that time, but never before did I feel the connection to a song in this way before. I felt overcome with power and emotion and could not hold back. I was not sure what all that meant, but I could not get those lyrics out of my head.

After the service, I walked into the premarital counseling class alone, constantly looking back at the door, hoping Matthew would walk in at some point to show me he still cared about saving this relationship. He never did. At the end, I was able to open up to the pastor and his wife about the struggles we were going through. He had known Matthew and his brother for a long time, but only just recently met me in passing and at the first class. After I let them in a little bit, he prayed over me. No one had ever prayed for me out loud before. It was unknown to me, and I would have normally thought it was strange, but his words that day were almost as powerful as the song lyrics I had just heard a couple hours earlier, and more tears came rolling out. How could someone who barely knew me know exactly the right words to say and pray about out loud? Was God speaking though him to me that day as well?

Once I got to my car, I did the same thing I do anytime I hear a song's lyrics which move me and found it on my streaming service. This time, however, it wasn't some song about some abusive guy or a break up song that I could listen to over and over, knowing I am not the only one out there being mistreated. This was a song about God! It gave me a different kind of strength and connection. I had never downloaded a Christian song before, but I must have listened to it at least forty times that first day, and the next, and so on and so forth. It was on repeat in my car to the point where my kids yelled at me to please change the song. I even played it on repeat one time I was hiding out in the bathroom away from Matthew that last week.

But I needed to hear those words over and over again. "I am a child of God. Yes I am." I was not a moron or a whore, or any of horrible names Matthew had called me that were engraved in my mind. If the highest, most almighty being out there, loved and accepted me for who I was, whether that was a kind and compassionate person at times or someone who drank too much wine and stumbled home from a neighbor's house, then why should I settle for anything less from anyone else? This Father was not going to abandon me or hurt me or call me names. He still loves me no matter what I do, and I have His grace and forgiveness always.

His love is unconditional and irrevocable and never-ending. He won't keep bringing up old sins, mistakes, or things I didn't even do wrong over and over. He forgives me and continues to love me with all of Himself. He sent his only Son to this Earth to die for me. What greater love is there? Would Matthew have died for me? He was willing to let our dog die to control me and get me back to the house to prevent me from making him look bad by not coming to church with me. Why had I put all my being and energy into him and not this God who loved me no matter what I did?

I don't have to walk on eggshells with Him. I don't have to explain every single thing I do and where I am and at what time and who I am with. He trusts me because He knows me and He knows my heart. I don't have to explain why I am who I am or why I forget things, or why certain things upset me, or why I have an attitude sometimes if I've had a bad day. He does not project upon me all of the traits He hates about Himself, like lying and manipulation. No, because He is perfect. He only projects endless love and care upon me! He doesn't make me feel guilty if I do not do something correctly or mess up or forget to do something. He continues to love me. He loves me not only in spite of all my shortcomings, but because of them too! He loves me for who I am, who I was, and who I want to be—no more, no less, at any time. A truly perfect and unconditional love. How much more amazing of a gift to receive!

It didn't take long for me to realize that I didn't have to be treated how I was being treated anymore. I finally started allowing God to do His work and realized the answers to my prayers about getting Matthew help were working, but they did not include me. I needed to be out of the picture before that happened because I was blinding him from reality. Matthew finally left me about a week later. I also realized I needed just as much help as Matthew, and it wasn't just him who had issues that stemmed from the pain of childhood trauma. I had them as well. I needed to allow God to do His work in me, and that also was not possible if we were still together. We fell victim to the world's mentality where two people come together to "complete" each other, when really, we each need to be our own complete person before we can come together and be one even greater person in God. We sought in each other to fulfill holes only God, self-love, and recovery work could.

The ensuing weeks were extremely difficult and felt almost impossible to get through at times. Away from me, I finally saw the man I originally fell in love with, gentle and kind, sweet and loving, to those around him. He seemed so happy and free now. Why couldn't he be that way with me? There was a lot of back and forth between lovingly separating and communicating, to no communication at all and the hurt that ensued from that. Friends stepped in on both sides and said it was best to not communicate at all, but I found myself in greater pain by not having that connection anymore, especially because I was not experiencing the abuse anymore and only saw the guy I had originally fell in love with and wanted that man again.

With as much support as I had from friends and family, it wasn't until after I met with my pastor that I had the wake-up call that I needed to let go of this person who could not love me how I deserved to be loved. He stopped me after an hour of detailing our relationship and asked, "Ellie, do you have any idea how many times you said 'I'm sorry' in the last hour?"

"Oh gosh, I am sorry," I replied back.

Apparently, it was a classic sign of being an abuse victim. I had no idea I was even saying it. It was so evident that I had been endlessly blamed for things over the course of the last two years that it became second nature to me to just apologize for general communication or just being me. It finally occurred to me that I didn't need to apologize for being myself, and that I was an incredible creation of God's, and He loved me for being me.

The second wake-up call which came from our conversation was when he asked me at the end, "Ellie, why would you ever want to get back with him?" I had been asked that question many times in the past by friends and family, but it didn't resonate until the pastor asked. I knew the answer in my heart, the same thing I believed about Matthew from the beginning of our relationship, but it didn't seem like he would take my answer seriously after everything I had just told him. I saw the man Matthew could be and who I knew he was deep inside. Unfortunately, he couldn't himself see that and projected his negative beliefs about himself onto me, which was a hard pill to swallow. My pastor told me I may be losing someone I loved but could not love me properly, but instead, I had gained someone who loves me not based on my perfection or performance in life, but based solely on Christ's perfection, which never changes. I could finally rest in peace with the knowledge and trust in that.

I walked out of his office that day in October and have had a smile glued to my face almost every day since. I was not alone, I was not unloved, I was not worthless, and I was worthy of the constant joy and peace I would have with my sights set on God in accepting His love. To be able to let go of all the anxieties about the future and have complete trust in my Father that this is exactly where I was supposed to be right then and what He wants for me, I was beyond excited for what He had in store for me in the future. I was always scared I would never again have such a strong passion and love for someone as I did for Matthew, and that's probably why I tried to hold on for so long. But now I had someone whom I would be even more passionate about and have more love for, and that person was Jesus, and there is nothing better in the world than the complete confidence, knowing I am being taken care of. His arms will hold me tight anytime I need. I do not have to worry about if I did or said something wrong that night.

From that point on, I started putting God as the number one person in my life and centered my life on the life Jesus lived so I could, in turn, walk His path right beside Him. Since putting Him first and accepting His love, I was, in turn, able to love myself as He does, which had a ripple effect on everything else in my life I had always struggled with. All of a sudden, things started getting easier. Since putting God first, I found my schedule opened up to make time for self-healing, codependent recovery work, immersing myself in the Word and self-help books that center around Bible-based therapy.

Church, which was once a chore, became my favorite activity of the week, and I couldn't wait for Sundays. I joined any classes they had available that day, and when I found myself slipping in the middle of the week, I ended up joining a women's Bible study group, and the people I have met through that have impacted my life in so many ways. Where I once was constantly stressed and hardly had any free time, I now had what seemed like endless free time to focus on what truly mattered in life, and the peace that arose from that is indescribable. Where I once devoted endless amounts of time and energy and literal blood, sweat, and tears on a romantic relationship, I instead started devoting that time to strengthening my relationship with God, and in turn, it flowed into relationships with others effortlessly. I have become a better mother, friend, daughter, sister, boss, ex-wife, and stranger to those around me.

With this new love I had accepted from God and, in turn, flowed through me, I started thinking of my heart and my body in a new and different way. I needed to guard them out of respect for not only myself, but for the Holy Spirit that dwells inside. I have been able to learn what boundaries actually are and how to enforce them. I realized all the times I tried escaping Matthew by going to my bedroom, or going for walks, were all attempts at setting boundaries. Without my self-love, I accepted him not only disrespecting them, but taking a truck and bulldozing them down to get to me.

It wasn't just Matthew I had a boundary-setting problem with, but all of them. Whether I initiated things or not, I was not guarding my heart or my body because I was so desperate for love that I accepted sex instead. For thirty-six years, God watched and waited patiently for me to realize I had this love the entire time. Anytime I thought He abandoned me or wasn't listening and I gave up on Him,

He did not turn away from me but instead waited patiently, planting seeds in my life to build up to this moment of salvation. Shortly after I met with my pastor, I had gone out on a date, and for the first time ever, I told a man *no*, and I didn't feel guilty about it at all. In fact, I felt even more loved because I knew I was loving myself as my Father was. I know there are men out there who will respect my boundaries, and even though it can feel lonely at times, I know it will feel even worse to lose my sense of worth and self-love again all for a brief moment of togetherness from someone who gives me false love.

CHAPTER 15

What Is Happening Here?

Sunday, November 21, 2021

Something is happening to me. Something new. It's really weird. Why don't I have a pit in my stomach anymore? Where has my anxiety gone? What is this overwhelming feeling I constantly have? Work was just really horrible and stressful…a dog literally died in my arms today. Died before the owner could get there, and I was the one to hold him for his last breath and for the next hour until she could get there. Why didn't I come home and pop Xanax and a bottle of wine? What is this calmness I have about me? Why didn't I yell at Greg for breaking my favorite glass the other day? I just had a really rough day. Why am I thanking God at the end of the night for it? Why am I driving alone in my car and tears start to come pouring out of me…but I have a big smile on my face so they are tears of happiness? That's never happened before! Why am I not crying anymore every night without Matthew in my arms? Who is this new man that has all my attention? Did I really just thank God for the pain and suffering I endured the last two years with a huge smile on my face?

Wait, did I just tell Kayla I could not attend her soccer game Sunday morning because I had to go to church? A few months ago, I told people I didn't need to attend church to have a relationship with God, and the whole institution is just wrong. Since when is she not no. 1 in my life, and since when would I chose something so "boring" over cheering on my daughter? Where's my rap music? Why are the last twenty songs I downloaded about Jesus? How am I supposed to booty shake to that? Did I really become one of "those" people who hold my arms out while the church band is playing a song? I was so embarrassed by those people a few months ago! Am I crying during the song out of happiness again? What happened to my infamous "wild Wednesdays?" Late nights out at the bar, trips to NYC or Philly to see a guy, etc. Did I actually just replace them with Wednesday night women's Bible study? Am I not going to be hungover at work the next morning? What will that feel like? Wow, these women are actually really fun. I can't wait to go back next week!

Did I just tell a guy no? Wait, why don't I feel guilty about it? I owed him something, didn't I? Why don't I care about their approval anymore? I need to fit in, right? Why don't I care at all about what they think? Did I actually just tell a gorgeous guy I will no longer be giving my body away anymore without the intent to marry, and not even apologize about it? I could just lie and say I was seeing someone else. That would have been way less embarrassing.

Why don't I watch TV anymore? I used to love the reality TV dating shows. I even once compared myself to the main girl when I was dating several guys at once! It was a game I used to play. Why can't I stand it anymore? I was even on a reality TV show once, kissing one of the main characters and getting drunk and dancing on tables for all to see. What the heck? I am going to do my Gospel class homework instead. Whoa…I am actually excited to go up to bed and read about the Gospel. Let me email my church group to get a conversation going about it. I always get really excited when I get emails from them or anyone at the church for that matter. Ugh, the variance for my detached garage just got rejected because of a spiteful jerk in my neighborhood. Why didn't I curse him out on the way out the door? I've been working on this for months and spent $1,500 on this application process. Why did I just smile at him and keep my mouth shut? Did I really pray for him last night? What is wrong with me? I should be asking karma to get him back. I was the spiteful and resentful one a few months ago.

Where's my running music? Going to be doing the six miles around Peace Valley, I think I am going to listen to the book of Matthew again instead. It's my favorite. Did I just talk about Jesus to my friend for thirty minutes straight at Chickie's at the bar? I did body shots on top of this bar a few years ago. Men literally took shots out of my belly button on top of this bar, and now I am talking about Jesus to them. Is there anything more opposite? I keep talking about God in front of my friends. That is not cool. I said my whole life "politics and religion are two things people shouldn't talk about in front of others." What a hypocrite! Oh well, I don't really care though! I have to hear about all the horrible things going on in this world constantly that people just love to talk and complain about. Why can't I talk about some good news! Covid, masks, politics, wars, labor shortage, rapes, murders, shootings—why do I have to hear all about that, but people don't want to hear about loving your neighbor as yourself? If we all just followed that basic premise, wouldn't the world be just about perfect? I don't get it. It sounds so simple and easy and wonderful! Did I just spend half an hour on the church website looking up ministries? Why wasn't I navigating Facebook instead? I am volunteering to freeze my butt off for three hours every night to be part of the Live Nativity production. This is craziness.

Who am I? Why do I feel so different? It's kind of exciting, I don't know… I feel like I am "coming out" as a new and different person. What are people going to think? Will they mock me? I certainly did… Wow, this must be a similar struggle to people going through other kind of lifestyle changes when they struggle with coming out. I think the world is more open to that kind of stuff nowadays than this though. It seems like it's more normal to start asking people to refer to one as they/their than to come out and say, "I want to walk with Jesus!" Why is it so frowned upon? Why are they taking God out of the school system? Better yet, why aren't there more classes out there on loving each other well? Shouldn't that be the most important lesson we learn in life? I guess it's just something I will have to endure. Because I do, and I am. I'm still me. I am not too different. But for the first time ever, I am whole.

*****

I wrote this journal entry on the day I attended a baptism class at church and decided I needed to become baptized to solidify my walk with Jesus. The day I decided to walk into that class, a woman said hello to me and told me we were old neighbors. Fifteen years prior as newlyweds, we knew each other but she had moved away, and I hadn't seen or talked to her in that time. I learned that she had been in an abusive marriage, had a special needs son, and also came to Christ recently. We were about to make these journeys together. Looking back fifteen years ago, neither one of us would have ever thought, in a million years, we would be in that room, in that church together, going through what we were going through, but this just attests to the miracle of God's plans for us coming to fruition and how He's known all along, planting people and experiences for us since before we were even born, even when we've thought He didn't care anymore. Now I couldn't imagine my new life without her.

Coming to Christ can be full of emotions, questions, and confusions. I don't like to call it a struggle because it is truly the most amazing experience and feeling I have ever been through. The struggle lies in realizing the death of your old ways of living, even if you knew it was bad for you. The struggle lies in having your eyes and ears open for the first time to the world around you and how broken and destructive it really is. The struggle lies in realizing most of us probably aren't going to heaven, including our family and friends whom we love very much. The struggle lies in sometimes realizing how our families of origin really messed us up and almost sets us up for failure in many areas of life. The struggle lies in the ways of the world constantly testing you and trying to pull you back with constant temptation. Realizing we are not in control of any of it, however, helps me get through it. Making the decision to be baptized in full submersion symbolized the death of my old life and ways and the resurrection of my new life, walking right beside Jesus on this new path in these new ways. I was completely settled and at peace with this "coming out."

It had been a few months since I came to Christ, and I was at a place in my life that I was so comfortable and happy with just being one with myself and God. I started thinking about Matthew less and less, and even though we saw each other at church from time to time, I no longer felt awkward or anxious about it. We both were healing, and I felt genuinely happy he seemed like he was in a good place. I decided I was ready to start dating again and met someone who was kind, sweet, cute, emotionally healthy, and most importantly, a Christian. It was hard not to think about Matthew as I sat across from this stranger each time, but I kept telling myself I needed to give this relationship a try. Maybe it didn't have the passion and attraction I had with Matthew, but maybe God was telling me there were sacrifices I needed to make to have an emotionally healthy and godly relationship.

Several weeks went by, and I went through the motions of Christian dating, which is completely different than the kind of dating I did before I met Matthew. I kept my sights focused on God though and did not sacrifice any of my activities or thoughts even on this new guy. Of course I didn't know it at the time, but looking back, I think this was one of God's tests to see if I was really serious about putting Him as number 1 in my life and not being overtaken by the excitement of a new relationship. It is easy to say God is our number 1 when we do not have anyone else to focus on, but if we think we are ready to practice what we preach, then He will give us a test for that. I think I passed with Joe, but maybe I still wasn't quite ready for the next guy he had for me, someone more familiar.

It was the first night of the Living Nativity our church puts on every other year. It is an enormous event with over ten thousand people in attendance over four days, and it would be my first time seeing or participating in it. Two years ago, Matthew was part of it, but I did not even go to support him. The thought of walking out in the freezing cold instead of holiday parties with friends sounded ridiculous to me. This year, of course, was much different, and I couldn't be more excited to be part of it.

At the end of the first night after four performances, I was leaving when I saw him at the door and said hello. We hugged and caught up for a few minutes, and as I was standing there talking to him, I realized I didn't feel anything for him romantically, just simple joy from what we had just accomplished. On the way home, I didn't think about him at all, except for the weirdness I felt not thinking about him in that way. Was I finally over him?

I was on a new high the rest of the weekend. Seeing the power of God work to bring all these people out to experience the story of the birth of Christ and the true meaning of Christmas, and seeing the lives that were touched by our performances and the pastor's message, was extremely overwhelming and full of intense emotions. I was so distracted by all of that I barely spoke to Joe that weekend. Putting God first was more important than anything because I knew the magnitude of people this one event could reach and knew they would be more open to listening to the message since it was Christmas time and it was presented in a beautiful and fun manner.

The final night of performances I was only signed up for the first three out of the four because I knew I would be freezing and tired. It was the coldest night out of all of them and so windy. I came back in, proud yet relieved my duty was finished ready to give my costume to the woman who had been patiently waiting in the room for her turn to go. "I think you should do this last performance," she said to me.

"Oh no, it's ok, you have been waiting, I am really fine with being done, I insist," I responded.

"I really just think you should do this one. I will be fine here." She rebutted. There was no convincing her, yet she was pretty convincing to me to do the last one.

At the very last scene we headed onto the risers around the manger scene while the wise men come up to give baby Jesus their gifts and then the pastor gives his message while everyone looked on at Mary, Joseph, and all the animals present. All of a sudden, I looked down, and to my surprise, Matthew was one of the wise men. He was on parking-lot duty that night. Why was he a wise man? Our eyes locked on each other, and it was at a powerful moment in the pastor's speech, and we just stared at each other and smiled for what seemed like hours but was probably no more than thirty seconds.

What was happening here? My heart felt like it melted into the rest of my body as a shock wave of warmth spread throughout, and I couldn't handle that feeling in that moment, because just three days prior, I felt nothing for him. That gaze. Those piercing eyes, it all came back to me from the first day we met and locked eyes across the room at that banquet hall. This was a different feeling though. It wasn't a "I have to have that man" feeling. It was more like "Look at where we are on this night, with this incredible full moon, in this nativity scene, the Lord all around us, and right in front of us. It was like we achieved a peace we both had longed for but couldn't achieve three months prior. Here we were, so much love for each other and our Lord and happiness for one another, knowing this is where we are at right now. Mentally speaking with each other, saying, 'Look around, this is where we are at right now,'" but not needing to because we were too fixated on each other.

Not being able to rationalize what was occurring inside of me, I immediately shifted my focus solely back onto the pastor and his message. When he had wrapped up, I fought to hold back tears on my way back to the changing room. I hurriedly made my way out to my car, hoping I could fight them long enough so no one would see me. For the next twenty minutes straight, I let all my emotions go and cried the entire ride home over the sheer power of everything I had just experienced that weekend and everything I was currently experiencing with the power of God and what this church had brought into my life. I was so proud of everything I had accomplished and so excited to see the ways in which God would use me in the future.

I wanted to text Matthew as I was getting ready for bed but wasn't sure if I should or what I would even say. I wanted to share with him how amazing the event was and how grateful I was to be part of it. I started drafting a message when I received one from Joe. Joe! Oops, he had been texting me all weekend, and I had totally blown him off. I didn't mean to. I just had so much going on and on my mind. He commented on me ignoring him and proceeded to tell me this relationship wasn't healthy for him. I laughed to myself for a moment but went right back to texting Matthew when he had sent me over a message first about how happy he was that I had so many friends and family come out to support me. It all seemed to flow in a purposeful way as it was a perfect ending to a perfect weekend, and for the first time ever, I felt a complete and utter peace with Matthew, even though I didn't know what that peace meant.

CHAPTER 16

Reborn

January 16, 2022
Baptism day

Today is the first day of the rest of my life. I don't think I can begin to describe this day. God was all around me, in everything and everyone. From the moment I woke up, I started listening to *Redeeming Love* and in the forty-five minutes or so that I was listening, it happened to be at the part where Angel had finally accepted Christ into her life and walked to the front of the church to ask to be baptized. The author even went through the questions, and I got to feel what she was feeling, and it gave me the biggest sense of empowerment and excitement, and I was overcome with emotion and tears. Just to think of all the things that had to happen to get me to that exact point…it goes back farther obviously but joining women's Bible study at the point I did, reading the book of Hosea, telling Jan my story, having her recommend this book, me downloading it but not touching it yet because I was reading all the other self-help books first. Then when those were all caught up to me finally being like, "Okay, I guess I will start it even though I don't really read novels." Then starting it when I did. Then baptism being pushed back a week, and all the time that was allotted to me this week to listen to get to the exact point in the book where I was this morning…the day of my baptism. Amazing. And just for Angel and Michael to be where they are at in the book, living separate lives so that Angel can become her own person, find God, and let Him heal her and realize she needs to put Him as her center…it hits home.

Reading it these last few days, I have realized things. I am going to let go of trying to convince Matthew to somehow love me, accept me, and change what I believe he needs to change. I am going to just love him as I know, even if that love means letting him go right now. He needs to heal a lot. More than me. He doesn't even know what his flaws are and that has been evident in our communication, so how can he begin to heal if he cannot acknowledge or accept what he actually needs to work on. He cannot do any of that still being attached to me. I've known it all along. But selfishly, I've clung onto him, knowing I want him and thinking we belong together and just wanting that now. But I have to be patient. He's not ready to love me how I deserve to be loved; he may never be. God has been telling me that, and I haven't wanted to listen. Because I thought I needed him. But needing him as a broken individual will do neither of us any good in the long run. Two complete people are needed to become the one that God intends them to be. Two incomplete people cannot complete one another. That is a recipe for disaster because we are constantly looking at that other person to fulfill what is missing within us, and they cannot do that, only God can.

Anyway, after listening this morning, I realized I really did want him by my side. Nothing I ever considered, and when he called me to ask me the other day, I didn't really think before I answered. And after I said sure and we hung up, I had many thoughts come into my mind. It just didn't feel right, him asking me. I didn't know what his motives were. Was it to try and be in control of the situation or put on a front, showing people he was by my side so he was this great guy who was fine with everything? I don't know. I knew what my family and friends would think, and I was worried. When he came over Thursday and said he didn't think it was a good idea after all, I was relieved. But this morning, I woke up wanting something different. I realized he brought me knowledge of Christ. God used him to get to me in the only way He knew I would listen, and because I did listen to Matthew, I did have that basic understanding of everything. So I wanted him there for that reason, and no other and I knew it was right. I couldn't find him though when I got there. I texted him but no response. I worried he saw the video in the 8:00 a.m. service and got mad and left. I couldn't help but think about it, but I mostly stayed focused. I knew he would be there with me, beside me, in spirit. So many others came…nineteen in total, and many others watched from home, fourteen more. Most of them nonbelievers. Maybe more to come…I am so blessed. After the service, there were lines of people coming up to me, congratulating me. One man cried as he told me how special I was and how impactful my testimony was and how happy he was that I am here and how good things will come. Overwhelmed does not even begin to describe what I am feeling. And then the responses on my post last night. I shared "What is happening with me?" with the Facebook world. I didn't care. I want people to know. I don't even think I can begin to thank God for answering every prayer I had about today. It couldn't have been more perfect. I should go to bed now. Goodnight!

*****

After the nativity event at the church, Matthew and I began talking again on the phone and through text. He told me he had been struggling seeing the kids and I and all my friends and family who came to the event. The holidays were fast approaching, and we knew we'd each be struggling with missing each other. It was so nice being able to have conversations without it leading to fighting. I began to think there may be hope for us in the future as it seemed we were both putting in the work to heal ourselves, and eventually, we could possibly come back together to work on the relationship.

He came over a couple times over Christmas week, including on actual Christmas, and even gave me a goodbye kiss on my lips. I was confused yet intrigued at the new feelings that began to form again, but I just said my goodbye and tried not to let myself get too excited. It was hard not to talk to friends or family about what was going on because I knew what they would all say. I don't think any of them trusted me at where I was in my healing journey yet to listen to or support anything I was thinking.

We made it through that week to New Year's Eve when one inconsiderate response to a "Happy New Year's" text turned into a fight, which brought us back to four months prior, where it seemed like any progress we had made was all a lie, and it was clear neither of us had really changed. He was still filled with anger and frustration, and I still let my feelings and emotions control my reactions to how he treated me. All the "catching-up" and "on-the-surface" talk had blinded me once again and gave me another false hope that he had changed. We stepped back from communicating for a few weeks after that when I received a call out of the blue a few days prior to my baptism.

I had emailed him, giving him a heads-up that my testimony would be on the screen and how I mentioned being in an abusive relationship and if that would make him feel uncomfortable or not. It was my story to tell, but I still cared about him and didn't want my story to affect his relationship with the church. To my surprise, he asked if he could stand by my side during the service to support me. I was caught completely off guard and told him sure, but after hanging up, I immediately thought about how it probably wasn't a good idea. What were his motives? Was he trying to be in control of the situation and put out the image that he was supporting me so everyone could see that he really was a good guy, or did he actually just want to support me? I needed to ask him.

The next day, he came over and came to the conclusion himself that it probably wasn't a good idea and that we probably shouldn't be talking much at all anymore. I was relieved because I was nervous as to what his reaction would be if I tried to be the one to tell him no. I realized I was still being controlled by him, whether I tried to avoid doing so or not. I wasn't sure what the whole point of the call the day before had been as we already weren't talking. Was this the need to exercise more control over me? I was still letting him get to me. Was I getting anywhere with my recovery? Every time I thought I was getting somewhere, Matthew entered back into my life and either gave me hope or hurt, and I wasn't sure how to handle it. So much doubt entered my mind over the next couple of weeks, and I was back to riding the roller coaster of emotions over Matthew and his indecisiveness over what he actually wanted in and from me. I kept my focus on God and decided to trust Him. I knew He had not abandoned me my entire life and knew He certainly wasn't going to now. I had at least come that far.

He came over one day a few weeks later after speaking with our pastor and seemed angered. He had just been told he was giving me mixed signals, and he should probably seek counseling for his anger issues. Two hours of gaslighting and denial and several put downs later, I was finally cured of my blindness and saw the truth. Where I had always swept the blatant lies I actually heard him say in the past under the rug, I finally realized he had a problem, especially once he denied kissing me on Christmas. Deep down, I knew I wasn't a liar or a manipulator, but I never knew why he continued to believe it so much in me. It bothered me more than any of the names he called me, or even the physical abuse I endured. It had been the one-character trait I actually did love about myself, and if that was lost, I would be left with nothing, except absolute hatred and disrespect of myself.

Matthew was projecting. He had been for two-and-a-half years. I knew he had so much pain and trauma he was holding onto from his childhood, but I didn't realize he was actually the liar and the manipulator this whole time. He was unconsciously taking these traits he hated about himself, whether he was aware of them or not, and attributing them to me. Others had been warning me of his insincerity for a while, but I was blinded by the fantasy that he really was that same person on the inside that he portrayed to others on the outside. I figured if he could just be the man I knew he was with everyone else, with me, then it would be perfect and would be everything I had always dreamed of. It was all a lie though. The person he thought I was actually was him, and everyone else could see it but me. I saw in him what he wanted everyone else to see, and they all saw what he was like truly inside. Did this mean he was cheating on me the whole time as well? All those accusations I had to endure, was he actually sneaking off and meeting up with another woman? I will probably never know. Everything seemed like a lie at this point, and my trust for him had been lost for now, but it's because I remained trusting of God. Because I kept my sights focused on God throughout, and after our conversation, I was finally able to see again.

Unfortunately, gaining my sight back had allowed me to see I was not alone here, and there was an epidemic at hand with abusive men and women, liars, cheaters, projectors, manipulators, and narcissists. It is the kind of world we are living in right now, and the enemy wants us to be filled with pride so that we are blinded by the idea of getting help to overcome these traits and display genuine agape love for one another how God intended it to be. We have convinced ourselves that living in a fantasy world about the potential of what our situations could be is better than the unknown of what lies ahead in actual reality if we escape these situations. So many of us are so affected by childhood trauma. However good we think our childhoods were, we gravitate toward what is familiar because that is what is known and comfortable, however hurtful the situation. God shows us what is, but the enemy shows us what we want to see, and it's extremely deceitful. We are often blinded by promises of love and this ideal person they outwardly act toward others that we cannot see what is actually going on right in front of us.

Gaining my sight back now allows me to not only see people for how broken they really are, but it has also opened me up to many other realizations about my life. Alcohol is no longer a problem for me. More than the hangovers, the negative influence on my children, or the stupid decisions I typically make under the influence, what finally made me cut down tremendously was coming to the realization that I was using it to become someone I am not in whatever situation was presented to me, and that was me not loving or respecting myself. How could I expect authentic, healthy, and trusting relationships if I was not being my true authentic self by becoming this different person when I drank?

In the past, I needed it to turn into this grander version of myself. I needed to be more outgoing, flirty, and promiscuous. I never thought I had anything to contribute to a conversation or a relationship until I got alcohol in me. I transformed from the shy and reserved girl from middle school to a woman who got all kinds of attention from all different avenues, a woman with confidence and cheerfulness. Even if I couldn't contribute intellectually to a conversation, I could at least be funny and flirty, and they would like me that way. I used alcohol to give me courage to transform into the woman I thought I wanted to be and rather who I thought everyone else wanted me to be, instead of realizing the woman I really am, the woman God created, was more than good enough. And if I am not good enough as I am to others, then that is their loss because I know God loves me exactly as I am.

I also realized I was using it to run into a fantasy world from whatever problem was being presented to me at the time. If I had to see my dad, I needed to get drunk so I could forget he had an affair and walked out on our family. I could pretend for that moment that everything was back to normal. If I needed to have a good night with my ex-husband, I needed alcohol to clear my head of all the repulsive comments he had made in the past to me. If I was fighting with Matthew, I needed to get drunk so I could live in the fantasy world where I could speak up for myself, and we could have a normal conversation and be back to where we were the first night we met and were crazy about each other. If I had a really stressful day at work, I came home and "needed a drink" so I could temporarily forget how horrible my employees were, instead of thinking through actual solutions to the problem so I wouldn't have to come home the next day and repeat the same motions.

Now that Christ resides within me, I love myself enough to know I do have plenty to offer to people in conversations, at parties, or even at a bar, without needing alcohol to turn me into a different person. I don't want to be that person anymore. That person was addicted to unhealthy relationships, accepted sex when all she really wanted to was love, and had constant anxiety from never actually gaining real practical solutions to the problems in her life. Now instead of drowning myself in wine, I can bring my burdens to God and wait for Him to present me with these solutions so that the problems can actually go away and not linger with the constant cycle of drinking and anxiety. I know He gives me a permanent solution rather than a temporary fix. I don't need alcohol to give me confidence to speak to people. He gives me that confidence, and by trusting Him, I've learned I have an abundance of meaningful wisdom and knowledge I can share with people that I never even knew resided within me. All these years, I sat silent and never thought I was good enough to engage people. Now people come to me for insights and meaningful conversations. I am my best self at church, in Bible studies, and small groups because I am not drinking, and I am able to contribute intellectually, and the church leaders are going to use me to lead others when it is my time. Getting this affirmation directly from God each day from strangers, even at church, lets me know I have a greater purpose here than getting drunk and partying all the time. Church classes are my new "fun."

If I am going to have the opportunity to drink, I now think ahead about what my motives are for having it and make the decision based on that. If I feel like I "need" it to cope from a bad day, then I need to pray instead. If I am nervous walking into a party and feel like I have to gulp one down quick to ease my anxiety, then I need to grab water first. If I am going on a first date and don't know what I am going to talk about, then I need to take my time with the menu and let the conversation get started on its own. God gave me this body, mind, personality, and heart. He already knows I am good enough. Alcohol alters my perception of who I am and what my reality is, so nothing good can come from excess drinking because it is not the natural state of me and who God intends me to be like. It leads to drunk texting, fighting because of an increased emotional state, drunk driving, promiscuity, embarrassment experienced by children, and many other negative consequences. None of these ever produce any spiritual fruit, and while the temporary fix may feel good in the moment, I know the lasting effects of my excess drinking have only ever done damage to myself and those around me.

Since my eyes and ears have been opened, my relationships have changed with my parents. I know my mother has been in pain for so long. She resorts to alcohol for the same reasons I did and, therefore, cannot see her own pain and the reasons behind it. Her heart appears to be hardened and holds on to bitterness and resentment to things done to her in the past. I no longer crave her acceptance but instead know I cannot fix her, so in turn, I pray for her salvation so that she too can be free from bitterness and anxiety.

I have gotten to know my father for the first time in thirty-six years. He was never "religious," but somehow recently, we have been able to connect on a deeper emotional level. I can feel God is trying to work on him and sense he's open but doesn't know where to start. We no longer talk about work, money, or cars, but instead, we talk about feelings and our past. He opens up to me, and in turn, I feel safe to open up to him. In getting to know him, I realized I am so much like him. I thought I was my mother this whole time, but that was only because we became "friends" in my later years. I am actually more like my dad and sought partners who were like my mother. Matthew was my attempt at being with someone like her, and since I could never get her acceptance, I thought I could get it from him. Knowing about my family of origin and how they factored into my life allows me to break the cycles and start fresh with my children.

I am no longer worried about who I am going to end up in a relationship with. He could be in my life already, he could be from my past, or he could be waiting patiently in my future. This need I've had for a man since about fourth grade was replaced by my need for God, and I know only because of that He will provide for me all that I need. I know God has been waiting patiently my whole life for me to find Him, and I know Jesus is waiting for me in Heaven, preparing my spot there to be joined together for eternity as my groom there. He is the one man who has relentlessly pursued me, in hopes that I would love me as He does. Why should I expect anything less out of a partner in marriage? Why should any of us? We are all worth more than an abusive partner makes us out to be.

D and I have begun talking again, even though he still lives a couple states away, but now I am able to see him every once in a while, and our friendship connection is undeniable. It is funny how the tables have turned, and we are able to have full-fledged conversations about scripture and Christianity, and he almost has stepped back somewhat in his beliefs at this point. He has remained my confidant and source of information and advice, even though I don't always agree with his perspective on things. I no longer think of him in a romantic way, but there is definitely a sense of safety and peace knowing I can always call him any time of day if I need someone to be there for me.

His advice isn't always agreeable, but either way, it has an impact. Just the other day, we were talking about guys, and he told me I should just settle. I wasn't going to find some perfect fairytale man, and he's right in a way—no one is perfect except Jesus. But that doesn't mean I have to settle. I know now I would rather wait however long it takes for God to send me my perfect man than to end up with someone I couldn't be all the way happy with. I can be at peace in the excitement of waiting for Him to send me someone, rather than the feeling of hopelessness in waiting impatiently.

Two more men from my past recently came back into my life. Reed and Tristan, two men who were part of my life in and out for several years, I saw within a week of each other after about two years without seeing or speaking. I believe it was a test for me, and I almost failed, but I stayed strong. It felt good to see each of them again, both performing at their respective places, and being able to connect with our eyes and later through conversation in person and through text. The excitement was there, but the desire to be with them again did not overcome my desire to keep focused on my path. It was good to see them, I had a peace about it, and then I moved on.

Matthew and I still see each other at church each week, but there is a new sense of peace I have. There is no longer that hope of reconciliation I thought made me happy, or the anxiety of seeing him when we are supposed to be on a communication break. It's more of an indifference, knowing it is not up to me to make Matthew "see" his imperfections, and it certainly isn't up to me to make Matthew love me for who I am. He was so angered because the pastor tried to make him see as well, and in turn, he wanted to run and blame someone else. I realized if our pastor couldn't even make him see, then I certainly wouldn't be able to, and I could have spent the rest of my life banging my head against the wall back and forth. He would have to come to the realization on his own, only with the help of God.

He had no idea the potential I had within me the whole time to be the best version of myself, God's version. Partially because I had no idea of my own potential while I was with him. He could not see the real me, partially because I couldn't be the real me around him. Or maybe he did see my potential but purposely exercised control over me to keep me down so that I couldn't flourish in every aspect of my life because he was so terrified of me leaving him. I could spend my life analyzing and wondering, but I know now that will never get me anywhere, and it only takes me off the narrow path to which I belong. The good news is, God knows my potential, and He will use others to show me that potential and push me to take risks and live up to it. Because I no longer make Matthew my god, the real God is allowing me to flourish in all areas of my life, and nothing, or no one, is going to stop me right now.

I think we get caught up with the hope that we can change someone by constantly drilling into their heads all they do wrong when the truth is, like the abuse victim, the abuser is also blind as to what they are doing. Their hearts are hardened, and they only see what they've manifested within their own heads about what they think of themselves. They need more prayers than the abuse victims themselves sometimes, because if they think they need to treat us the way that they do, that just means that's how they think they deserved to be treated. Now when I think of loving my neighbor as myself, I want to love them relentlessly as God does. Abusers do not know that true love and, therefore, have to treat ones they think they love as the awful people they think they themselves are. It pains me to realize and accept all my faults and flaws, but I also am blessed that I am able to work on them. Those who are unaware are going through life with broken relationships and will continue to be lost and broken until they have these realizations. All we can do is continue to love them and pray for them, and sometimes, that love means leaving them alone because we are the ones causing them to be blind.

The good news is, our God is relentless. He will not turn away when we have. He wants us to need Him and thirst for Him. He wants to be the one to fulfill us, no one else. If we are fulfilled by Him, then everything else will come in time. He loves us for who we are, who we were, and who we will be in the future, and there is no greater feeling of peace than finally knowing that. The other day, I took my old dog out, Chunk, and was watching him in the yard. Because he is blind, he does not always come back to the door after he goes potty. Sometimes he goes toward the road, sometimes he crashes into a few bushes along the way back, but he makes it, sometimes he ends up in a ditch, and sometimes he does make it back on his own. When he veers off his path, I have to go out to him and pick him up and bring him back. That is how God is with us. He allows us to walk the path, but sometimes we veer off course. We may bump into a bush or we may end up in a ditch. Either way, He will always come to us, put His arms around us in a loving grip, and bring us back home.

As people learn of my past, they sometimes cry for me and tell me how sorry they are. I stop them instantly and tell them to not feel sorry for me. I love my mother, my father, Eric, and everyone who has come into my life in between, whether positive or negative. I love Matthew more than anyone will ever understand. When I see them now, I see them as children as well. Innocent creations of God, marred by unfortunate circumstances throughout their own lives, trying to do whatever they can as a means for their own survival, without even knowing any hurt or pain they may be causing another.

I do not regret a thing that has happened to me whether someone else was the cause or I brought it on myself because it brought me to where I am at now. Sitting here feeling sorry for myself or letting others feel sorry for me will never get me anywhere. I have to acknowledge it, accept it, and use it. I finally know why that passage was given to me on the day of my salvation and why I felt compelled to write it down. It was tough going through school, bouncing around from group to group, never really having a particular clique. I know now it was for a reason. He has equipped me with certain gifts, certain circumstances, and certain people in my life so that I have the opportunities to become all things to all people so that I may spread the good news of Christ our Savior and what He's done for me. God allowed everything to happen to me throughout my life so that I could use my experiences to serve a greater purpose. His purpose. Because He is my Father, and I am His child.

ACKNOWLEDGMENTS

I would like to dedicate this book first and foremost to God. It is His story to tell, not mine, and I am eternally grateful to Him and His relentless love and pursuit of me. Next, to my neighborhood crew for always being there for me and being the wonderfully generous, fun, and crazy group that you are. To watch me grow over the years and then to be as supportive as you all are now, whether you believe it or not, I truly appreciate you. Then to my Women's Wednesday Night Bible Study crew. I have only known you a short time, but I am beyond blessed to have God's love working through all of you and shining it upon me. My mentor, for coaching me and never being afraid to give it to me straight and making me realize how important it is to be your true authentic self because no one is going to see God's glory if you keep those parts of you hidden. My pastor, for helping me realize not only my potential but just how much God really loves me and really being the guiding force to help me through such a difficult time. Thank you for putting up with my hour-long responses to simple questions and my enormous personality that continues to grow each day. Truly though, your passion and zest for life and the Lord has been an amazing inspiration for me. To Living Hope Community Church, for being a place that brings me pure joy and peace just by being inside the doors and the vessel for bringing me to Christ. For being the community of imperfect people that you are, who truly accept any and all, and have welcomed me from the very beginning even if it looked as though it was the last place I wanted to be. The rest of my friends, you know who you are. J, for our daily talks on the phone on your way to your second job and having to listen to all the details of all my relationships over the years and never judging me for my decisions. S, my friend since preschool. Truly living this entire story with me throughout my life and just being that friend I could not talk to for two years and then one of us picks up the phone, and it's like we just talked yesterday. To my mom and my dad, you guys truly did an amazing job raising us, and I can't ever thank you enough. You aren't perfect, and that is okay. I still love you so much. And to my brothers. Having you guys around got me through some really tough times in life, and I love all the memories we created as kids. My sisters-in-law, thank you for just wanting me to be happy. To E, thank you for your patience, calmness, love, and support over the years. You are my best friend. K, you are the best daughter one could ask for. Your kindness and care for others is something I look up to. And G, my buddy, I know how frustrating it could be not being able to communicate with people, but you are the happiest kid I know and truly a testament of how others should live despite their limitations. Finally, M, without you I may never have come to Christ. I know it wasn't in the way that either of us wanted, but nevertheless, you provided me with some foundation that He would later use and I will forever be grateful.

ABOUT THE AUTHOR

Elaina resides in Bucks County, Pennsylvania, and is the mother of two amazing children, two dogs, and two guinea pigs. Her first passion is Christ, and she serves faithfully in various leadership roles in her church, along with community outreach. Her lifelong love for animals, combined with her passion for leadership and entrepreneurial spirit, led her to open her own pet hotel and grooming facility in her young twenties, which she continues to operate with great success. When she isn't busy lavishing attention upon each of her canine companions, you can find her attending her kids' extracurricular activities, taking walks around local parks, watching live music, or simply enjoying her yard. She is an avid board-game enthusiast and enjoys hosting game nights with friends, where you will often find her laughing uncontrollably at the silliest things. She loves all things outdoors—hiking, fishing, golfing, going to theme parks, and simply curling up on her back deck with a good book. She enjoys traveling anywhere from the beach to the mountains, or simply visiting family in order to escape the chaos of everyday life and focus on her writing—another passion of hers since she was about ten years old. She currently leads an adult single's group at her church, focused on helping others grow in emotional health and spiritual maturity, and is dedicated to providing support to those on both ends of abusive relationships. Her goal is to share the gospel on a daily basis, in hopes that others will experience all of the love and joy that Christ has brought into her life.